Filthy Fishermen is a ... is offensive to the righ... captivity. I believe God will use this book to radically impact the church and help transform church culture into something real, raw, and powerful. Dr. Luke has an amazing testimony that I can relate to on many levels, and it encourages me to see young filthy fishermen become champions of God!

—TOMMY "DEBO" LISTER
ACTOR

Dr. Luke brings some amazing revelation on the heart of the Father in his new book, *Filthy Fishermen*. It is a book that I believe is a love song to the world and to the church. It shows that all of us can, at some time, become wayward children looking desperately for a way back home. This message of grace is freeing and well balanced. I highly recommend this book.

—MIKE JAMES
NBA STAR

Dr. Luke's new book, *Filthy Fishermen*, gives us an astounding and encouraging look into the heart of Jesus. I highly recommend you read this book and take the time to let it sink deep into your heart. You will be inspired to share the redemptive love of Jesus with everyone around you. It will open your eyes to the power of God's love for humankind. Within these pages, you will be challenged to become a true fisher of men.

—BOBBY CONNER
AUTHOR, PROPHET, AND FRIEND

God uses ordinary people to do extraordinary things! This is a phrase I often use in my messages to bring hope, restoration, and vision to God's champions who may not yet recognize their destiny and purpose. Dr. Luke Holter has done an amazing job capturing that truth and conveying it in his new book, *Filthy Fishermen*. In this book you will see a chronicling of God's unconditional love, unmerited favor, and profound grace to save, deliver, and empower a generation of twenty-first-century champions. If ever there was a generation in need of hope, it is ours. Hopelessness is an epidemic, and the remedy can only be found in Christ Jesus. Luke takes us on that journey to discover hope, purpose, and fruitfulness. I believe with all my heart that this book will be a wonderful tool for freedom that will transform church culture, as well as those in the world.

—Paul Keith Davis
Author and Evangelist

I have such an excitement in my heart for this book. One reason is because I know the life of the author! Prophet Luke Holter is not only a man of honor, but I also deeply believe he has his finger on the very pulse of God, the church, and the called. *Filthy Fishermen*—the title itself begs the reader to delve deeper! There is not a single person out there who has not made terrible mistakes.

After traveling the world declaring the freedom Christ brings for nearly two decades, I have come to realize that the ones who are being greatly used by God are usually the ones with the deepest scars. These are the ones who have made up their minds that their scars end where Christ's scars begin. These are the ones who understand that with great pain we must have great compassion. I believe God especially uses the broken and desperate, because without Him their stories would end differently. This powerful book will take you on a journey to understanding that God not only likes you, but He also is ready to empower you! Your failures are God's invitation to heal!

—Pat Schatzline
Author and Evangelist

I am in Luke Holter's cheering section as he releases *Filthy Fishermen* in this critical hour of reformation. It will empower you through grace and truth to raise the bar of your faith, your values, and your walk in Christ. I highly recommend this book for both personal reading and to use as a study tool in groups.

—Patricia King
Founder, XPmedia

To Debbie,

HOW GOD
USES WEAKNESS
FOR HIS GLORY

FILTHY
Fishermen

may you be blessed!

HOW GOD
USES WEAKNESS
FOR HIS GLORY

FILTHY
Fishermen

LUKE HOLTER

CHARISMA
HOUSE

Most Charisma House Book Group products are available at special quantity discounts for bulk purchase for sales promotions, premiums, fund-raising, and educational needs. For details, write Charisma House Book Group, 600 Rinehart Road, Lake Mary, Florida 32746, or telephone (407) 333-0600.

Filthy Fishermen by Luke Holter
Published by Charisma House
Charisma Media/Charisma House Book Group
600 Rinehart Road
Lake Mary, Florida 32746
www.charismahouse.com

Unless otherwise noted, all Scripture quotations are taken from the Holy Bible, English Standard Version. Copyright © 2001 by Crossway Bibles, a division of Good News Publishers. Used by permission.

Scripture quotations marked MEV are taken from the Modern English Version. Copyright © 2014 by Military Bible Association. Used by permission. All rights reserved.

Scripture quotations marked NAS are from the New American Standard Bible, copyright © 1960, 1962, 1963, 1968, 1971, 1972, 1973, 1975, 1977, 1995 by The Lockman Foundation. Used by permission. (www.Lockman.org)

Scripture quotations marked NIV are taken from the Holy Bible, New International Version®, NIV®. Copyright © 1973,

Cover design by Studio Gearbox
Design Director: Justin Evans

Visit the author's website at www.lukeholter.org.

Library of Congress Cataloging-in-Publication Data:
Names: Holter, Luke, author.
Title: Filthy fishermen / by Luke Holter.
Description: First edition. | Lake Mary, Florida : Charisma House, 2016. |
    Includes bibliographical references and index.
Identifiers: LCCN 2015046414| ISBN 9781629986500 (trade paper : alk. paper) |
    ISBN 9781629986517 (e-book : alk. paper)
Subjects: LCSH: Redemption--Christianity. | Providence and government of

God--Christianity. | Failure (Psychology)--Religious aspects--Christianity.
Classification: LCC BT775 .H65 2016 | DDC 234--dc23
LC record available at http://lccn.loc.gov/2015046414

Some names and identifying details have been changed to protect the privacy of individuals.

16 17 18 19 20 — 98765432
Printed in the United States of America

DEDICATION

To MY WIFE.

When I look at everything God has spared me from, I see it all illuminated by the warmth of the eyes of my wife, Grace. She really has been a manifestation of her name in my life. I found her when my heart and faith were both shipwrecked on the rocky shores of circumstance and personal failure. Somehow she saw past my weakness and saw me as a much greater man than who I felt myself to be at that moment. Yes, I was and am completely out of my league when it comes to my wife.

I had a dream about her in the sixth grade. In it I was getting married to a short Asian woman in a wedding dress. When I was thirty years old, I saw her across a crowded room at church. Believe it or not, telling someone, "I dreamt I married you," isn't the best opening line—unless of course you're in Bible college.

I worked up the nerve to go talk to her, and I discovered she is amazing. Breathtaking. She was everything I wasn't at that time. I measure every pain and disappointment from past mistakes against those warm brown eyes that welcomed my company. I fell in love with the woman I had been praying for all those years, even while I was lost in drug addiction.

After a few dates the Lord told me, "Tell her everything about your past, and hold nothing back."

I began to shake, and my stomach turned. I said, "No! That isn't fair, God! She will leave me."

He then said, "Baby boy, it's unfair to have her fall in love with you, and then make her deal with your past failures. If you truly love her, you will give her the choice before she's trapped in the throes of love."

So I did. I told her everything, and all she could do was sit there and weep. I thought to myself, *She's grieving the loss of what she had hoped for in a husband.* I waited through twenty minutes of silence as she sat crying.

Then I said, "Would you say something? Tell me you hate me or you never want to see me again."

She looked up at me with her big, brown eyes and tears rolling down her cheeks and said, "I'm the luckiest girl in the world."

Grace—this book is for you. I love you more than I could ever possibly show or say. But I know this for sure—I am going to spend the rest of my life trying.

CONTENTS

Part 2
LOVE LIKE A HURRICANE

ACKNOWLEDGMENTS

Special thanks to God, Jesus Christ, the Holy Spirit, Grace Holter, Gemma Holter, Barry and Cheri Holter, Mike and Joy Myers, Mark and Jeannie Holter, the Laurels, the de Castros, Virginia and Jon Plaisance, the Manitos, Shawn and Cheri Bolz, Mike James, Tommy "Tiny" Lister, Pat Schatzline, Bobby Conner, the Humphries, the Martinez family, Darin Crawford (outstrengthed), the Caldwells, the Beckers, the Wagners, the Laughlins, the Baerg family, Jerry Heartless, Dr. Richard Heard, Andrew Heard, the Nowlings, Sean and Angela Jackson, Daniel and Mary Beth Rose, David and Janice Betzer, Patricia King, Stacy and Wesley Campbell, Paul Cain, Bob Jones, Don and Susan Nordin, 8 Bit Nintendo, Bishop Bill Hamon, Jerame Nelson, Bill Johnson, Reggie Dabbs, Rich Albrecht, Angela Albrecht—and the entire Albrecht clan.

FOREWORD

GRACE IS AN AMAZING THING. THE FACT THAT our God recreates destiny and, as Luke puts it, restores us so completely that it seems like we never needed restoration is amazing. I know Luke Holter very well, and when you know someone who is being perfected by love and grace, it is hard to imagine his life outside of it or his past. Luke is such a strong man that grace hides his past, and even when he tells us the crazy stories of his life, it's like watching a movie—surreal, no longer real. His life is truly reshaped.

Luke shares from his own vulnerability, telling the

story of his past, and then shines a vulnerable light on many of our biblical heroes. He helps us see that the most beautiful part of God is a love that wants us and longs for us to be like Him and in Him. He is a God who never stops chasing us or planning the highest for us, even if we turn our hearts away.

I am convinced that if Judas had not killed himself, Jesus would have run after him after the Resurrection. Jesus never surrounded Himself with enemies or "frenemies." He chose to believe the best in each one of those He spent time with. He called them true friends. Even when He said, during the great Last Supper, that one of the twelve would betray Him, He also told Peter he would deny Him three times. Peter and the other disciples could tell Judas was becoming a prodigal and probably had religious judgment toward him for how he was handling money and power. But Jesus put even Peter on the same playing field of betrayal while still speaking promises over all of them. If Judas hadn't died, Jesus would have gone to him right after He found Peter, because He returned to all who betrayed Him, and His love and sacrifice were big enough to cover any betrayal.

Many people who have a prodigal heart commit spiritual suicide because they believe God could never love them again. Luke helps us to see that God never changes, even when we do. He is fully ready to embrace and love in an unhuman way, taking the weakest people in the world and making history with them.

This book will help many people see their value again, just as Luke is now fully released back into destiny and isn't limited by his past. Christianity is the only place where people can experience that kind of full restoration, where their weakness becomes a badge of honor for what God can do.

As we enter into this new harvest field, many people will look unrecoverable. Many will look unworthy, too. But God is going to catch the farthest gone people and raise them up to be champions of His love.

—Shawn Bolz
Senior Pastor, Expression58
www.expression58.org
Author, *The Throne Room Company,*
Keys to Heaven's Economy,
and *The Nonreligious Guide to Dating*

INTRODUCTION

I KNOW IT MIGHT BE HARD TO BELIEVE, BUT YOU did not invent failure. And you are not the definition of failure either. Failure has been around since the beginning of time. Remember Cain? Only a small number of people lived on Earth, and he just happened to be the murderer. But what we always forget is that God vigorously protected and defended this murderer. God marked Cain—not because he was a murderer but to protect him from anyone who would try to kill him. In the aftermath of Cain's malevolent deed, God responded by making him a promise to protect him for the rest of his life.

What?

Cain murdered his own baby brother out of jealousy, and God promised to protect him forever? That's incredibly offensive to all our notions of justice, law, and punishment. But that's the economy of God.

And that's what this book is about. Do not proceed if you are faint of heart. This message will ruin you for anything other than true Christianity.

I must confess that I am no stranger to failure. Those who have heard my story know my life has been very, very far from perfect. My life has been a beautiful kind of broken. I am a preacher's kid whose parents were told to have a funeral for me because it would be easier for them to deal with the pain of death than the pain of a living disappointment.

But God had another plan. God broke in.

THIS MESSAGE WILL RUIN YOU FOR ANYTHING OTHER THAN TRUE CHRISTIANITY.

This book is about healing, restoration, grace, and so much more. You will read my story, the stories of painfully real people who have become my friends, and the stories of the innumerable biblical forefathers who failed, failed again, failed some more, and then were redeemed and restored so extravagantly that it would offend any religious bone left in your body. You know you are in trouble when you are more religious than the Bible.

This book was both a painful and a healing book for me to write. I suppose it's never easy to relive your failures. Or perhaps it is the realization of just how incredible God is. Truly all things are possible with Him. And no beauty compares to the beauty God exchanges for ashes.

If you are wrestling with failure, this book is for you. If you are wrestling with hopelessness, this book is for you. If you are a parent or leader, and you've reached your wit's end, this book is for you.

Don't give up. Keep hanging on. I pray this book will help you to discover a God who really is love, healing, and hope; the One who never gives up.

—LUKE HOLTER

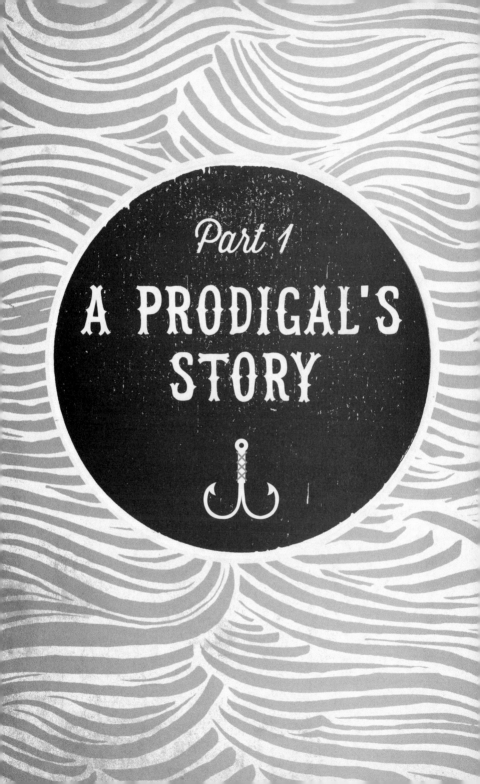

Part 1

A PRODIGAL'S STORY

Chapter 1

SOMETHING'S WRONG WITH MY HEART

I WAS TWENTY-FIVE AND DYING OF A HEART attack, with no one beside me but a redheaded stripper/witch whom I barely knew. I'd fallen off the stage, flat on my face, after my punk rock band hit its first note in the set.

As I lay there, my heart violently convulsing, the only one who came to my aid was Wendy, a girl I'd met the night before at a bar and invited to watch my band play. She was a practicing witch who stripped for a living.

Somehow, she was able to drag me up to the roof, where she offered up "good prayers" for me.

I then heard an audible voice speak to me. It was Satan, and he said, "You are going to die tonight." I believed the threat was very, very real.

Wendy dropped me off at the door of the ER, and I walked in screaming, "Something's wrong with my heart! Something's wrong with my heart!" After her short visit with me in the hospital, Wendy had to leave for work. When she was gone, I began to sob uncontrollably. Deep, gut-wrenching sobs resonated in my room as I lay there alone, with no one to call.

This was the end. I was alone, and I was going to die.

All I could think about was what a disappointment I had been to my parents and what a failure I was before God. I hated myself! I hated all the pain I had caused. I hated how I had shattered all my own hopes and dreams and squandered all my promise and potential. I was going to die alone, filthy and broken in my pigpen.

My name is Luke, and I was a prodigal in every sense of the word. I know what it's like to feel too far from home, redemption, and hope. I know what it's like to fear the morning because it means another day of failure and regret. I know what it's like to be filled with self-hatred and even to hate those who refuse to give up on you. I know what it's like to be so far removed from

God that any mention of His name brings immediate guilt, shame, and anger.

> JESUS ISN'T AFRAID OF FAILURES. HE EMBRACES THEM, AND HE REDEEMS THEM.

But I also know what it's like to be loved back from the brink of death—to be healed, restored, and redeemed to the point of offending the religious crowd. Offensive grace. Unthinkable mercy. Unexplainable love.

You see, Jesus didn't come for those who were well; He came for the sick, lost, and dying. He chose filthy fishermen and ruthless tax collectors to be among His closest friends. Jesus isn't afraid of failures. He embraces them, and He redeems them.

WRETCHED AND FILTHY

The day before my fateful heart attack, my parents paid me a surprise visit. This was always something I dreaded because of how I was living. Because of shame, I would go nine months at a time without speaking to them. They literally showed up unannounced at my front door.

"We were just passing through and wanted to stop by and let you know we love you and to make sure you are OK," they said.

I couldn't believe it. It was one thing for me to live

in filth, but it was another to have my parents see it. I didn't have time to hide anything from their wide-open eyes and hearts. It was too much to bear.

"Please don't look at me, don't look at what I'm doing. Please don't see me this way! Your little boy is still in here somewhere," I thought, pleading silently.

I immediately reverted to that broken little boy. I was so ashamed to let them see me living in filth. My apartment was full of pornography, drugs, alcohol, and drug paraphernalia. And there my parents were, standing at my living room door with nothing but love and compassion in their eyes. I stepped back and reluctantly let them come into my pain.

I could see them looking around, slowly, silently. They didn't comment on how I was living or why I couldn't just get it together. Instead, they offered to buy me groceries or take me to the doctor for a checkup.

My shame and pride were instantly triggered. I didn't want their help; I was fine! Instead, I bragged that my band was playing a big gig the next night and asked if they wanted to come. I wanted them to see that I was fine. Really, I was hoping they would see greatness in me while I was on stage, hoping I could make them proud again.

My parents declined, saying they could not stay in town but had to be on their way. As they left, my mom reminded me that she loved me and said people back home were praying for me. Then they were gone. Later, I found out that after leaving, my mom and dad went toe-to-toe with God and challenged Him on His promises. My mom said to God, "I give You permission to do whatever it takes."

That night I went to work at my overnight job unloading semi-trucks at a large supercenter. Because I was unaware of my mom's prayer, it seemed like any other night of work. But it was not going to be a normal night. While I was on the sales floor, standing on a ladder and putting away stock from the semi-truck, all of a sudden a feeling washed over me that I hadn't felt since the sixth grade at Bible camp. I immediately thought, "Well, this is it. I'm going to die." I was feeling the presence of God like I had during my spiritual encounters as a child, and I assumed that meant it was the end. Time seemed to slow, and my breathing became shallow. Then, all of a sudden, I felt a tap on my shoulder. I turned around and found myself eye-to-eye with an angel.

At that time in my life, I didn't believe in angelic activity. I thought that stuff had happened only in Bible times, and people who believed they saw angels today were probably just exaggerating. I viewed it as Christian folklore or superstition. Yet heaven was touching earth in a very real way at 2:00 a.m. in a supercenter. The angel was over nine feet tall and had bushy, white hair and a beard. He was also three dimensional, but he would switch to two dimensional without warning. He wore a black vest, grey shirt, and blue jeans—making him look very much like a biker Santa Clause. When the angel spoke, his voice had three octaves simultaneously, and

I knew instantly these were the Father, Son, and Holy Spirit in perfect harmony. If that wasn't crazy enough, the voice that came from the angel did not come from its physical body but from outside of time, where the Spirit hovers over the deep.

The angel's presence emanated—"Behold!" Then He said to me, "Can I ask you a question?"

"Yes," I said.

"When are you coming home?"

Immediately I thought of the verse that says Pharaoh hardened his heart (Exod. 9:34), and I turned around and said, "Whatever. Just leave me alone."

Internally I began praying to God that He would make the angel go away—which, believe it or not, doesn't work!

GOD'S WAITING FOR YOU TO RETURN.

Then the angel grabbed my shoulder. I saw things as he touched me. I saw him walking through Sodom and Gomorrah as fire fell. I saw him walking through Pompeii as ash covered people. His hand was so large His fingers came down the front of my chest and His palm was at the base of my shoulder blade. He spun me around and said, "You know who I'm talking about. God's waiting for you to return."

Everything around me moved so slowly that I felt as if time was standing still. The angel then walked away and turned a corner. I jumped down off my ladder right away to follow him, but when I turned the corner, I saw he was gone. My eyes began to well up with tears as I walked to the back stockroom. I looked toward heaven and said, "You're going to have to try harder than that."

That was a big mistake.

FAR FROM HOME

I can imagine the utter shame and humiliation of the prodigal son in Luke 15 after he had squandered all his inheritance. I suppose it's because I lived it for seven years.

At the beginning of the infamous story, we learn this young man was born into a wealthy family as the younger of two sons. He was entitled to a one-third inheritance of his father's estate according to Jewish tradition. Rather than wait for his father to die, however, the young man demanded his share of the wealth immediately.

"I want my share of your estate now, instead of waiting until you die," he says to his father. Incredibly, the father obliges his audacious younger son.

A couple days later, the young man "packed all his belongings and moved to a distant land, and there he wasted all his money in wild living" (Luke 15:13, NLT).

The son voluntarily went into exile, leaving God's

7

holy land and the moral standards of his fellow Jews. He went to live among the pagans, away from prying eyes, where he was free to live loosely and indulge his every desire. The Bible lists prostitutes among the son's selected indulgences (Luke 15:30). Why not? After all, he had no one to answer to.

After an extended time of heavy partying in his newfound land, after his inheritance was spent, a great famine struck, and the young man began to starve. He managed to find a job feeding a pagan farmer's pigs. Day in and day out he fed these filthy animals—pouring bucket after bucket of slop into their feeding troughs after slogging through their muddy, manure-filled pens. His hunger compounded with each passing day and became so severe that he began to develop an appetite for the very slop he'd been feeding to the pigs. But "no one gave him anything" (Luke 15:16).

Finally, the young prodigal became so desperate that he began to plot a way back home. Thinking his father would never receive him back as a son, he planned, "I will go home to my father and say, 'Father, I have sinned against both heaven and you, and I am no longer worthy of being called your son. Please take me on as a hired servant'" (see Luke 15:18–19, NLT).

The young prodigal, filled with hopelessness, guilt, and shame, believed he was as filthy on the inside as he was on the outside, and he believed he had squandered his identity along with his inheritance. After all, he was practically living in a pigpen!

And that was me—son of a king living in a pigpen full of sexual immorality, pornography, drugs, and drug paraphernalia. I was far from home. Very, very far from home. I had gone so far I didn't think I could ever come back—certainly not as a son. That's what I had learned from society, anyway.

But Jesus kept calling.

HOMECOMING

The one thing the prodigal son did not expect was a father who would welcome him home with open arms. Not after all he had done. Not after the way he had scorned his father. Surely he first needed to be punished before he could be let back in. And no way was he ever going to be treated like a son again.

So Jesus tells us the son came home to his father. But he didn't get the cold-shouldered homecoming he expected. Instead, while he was still a long distance away, his father saw him coming and, filled with love and compassion, he ran to his son, embraced him, and kissed him (Luke 15:20).

Who knows how long the father had been sitting, waiting, and watching for his son to return home. Perhaps since the day he left. In those days he couldn't text him or call him and had no way of knowing whether his son was alive or dead. What we do know is that the father didn't give up. Even if he had been angry with his son at some point, that didn't matter anymore.

The father probably couldn't believe his eyes when he saw his son coming. Finally! It was a miracle! He ran to his son and enveloped him in his arms, paying no mind to the layers of dirt on his skin, the stench of his hair, or his ratty attire.

And what did the son do? He stuck to his plan. His father was running to him, relentlessly hugging and kissing him, and all he could think about was how he had let his father down.

"Father, I have sinned against both heaven and you, and I am no longer worthy of being called your son," he lamented, unable to see himself as anything more than a failure (Luke 15:21, NLT). He was so disappointed in himself that he couldn't even receive his father's love and joy. As humans we tend to assume (wrongly) that because we are surprised by our failures, God is as well.

I love that the father responded by ignoring him. He didn't even acknowledge the self-loathing words coming out of his son's mouth. Still clinging to his son, the father turned to his servants and told them to bring the finest robe, sandals, and a ring, and to kill the calf they'd been fattening in the pen.

"We must celebrate with a feast, for this son of mine was dead and has now returned to life. He was lost, but now he is found" (see Luke 15:23–24, NLT). So the party began.

What a homecoming! I bet this party was better than any pagan party the son had ever been to. Who would've thought he would go from feeding pigs to being the guest of honor at an extravagant feast? And all he had to do was come home.

It didn't matter how filthy he was when he arrived home. His father didn't care what he had done before finally deciding to come home, or how much the stench of sin and the rot of ruin clung to him. It would not have mattered if he had run, walked, or crawled home. All that mattered was that he was home.

IF YOU ARE FAR FROM HIM, HE IS LOOKING FOR YOU, WAITING AND WATCHING FOR YOU.

Is the Father waiting for you to come home? Do you hear His Holy Spirit calling you home? The reality is, if you are far from Him, He is looking for you, waiting and watching for you. He wants to throw you a party, and He doesn't care how dirty you are; He's ready with new garments and a ring! And when He sees you coming, your silhouette peeking out over the horizon, He will run to you. He's been waiting—oh, He's been waiting!—to hold you, embrace you, and kiss you.

"Home! Home at last," He will cry over you as He clings to you. "Home! My baby is home at last!"

Chapter 2

BITTERSWEET DESTINY

ONE PARTICULAR MEMORY OF MY CHILDHOOD often surfaced during my prodigal years. I was five years old, and my family was headed to church bright and early on a Sunday morning. I was in the backseat, the windows were rolled down, and the sun was shining warmly on my face. I felt the comforting glow of life bearing down on me on an unadulterated and picture-perfect day. In that moment everything was right, and my life was perfect. Nothing seemed like it could ever go wrong.

This memory vividly flashed in my mind whenever my parents loved on me as a prodigal. I would feel like all was well with the world again because I was their little boy once more. I felt safe, secure, and happy. Then, in an instant, I would snap back to reality, and shame and bitterness would begin gnawing at my heart. These warm moments from my childhood were just distant memories from a life I'd let slip through my fingers. Hopelessness would come and overwhelm me, regret would fill my heart, and I'd turn back to my drugs and pornography to deliver myself from the sickening pains of grief in my stomach. And I would never know how I had gotten to the point where I had squandered literally everything away.

STABBING PAINS

A verse in the Book of Psalms evokes this same anguish deep in my heart, all these years later:

> My heart is breaking as I remember how it used to be: I walked among the crowds of worshipers, leading a great procession to the house of God, singing for joy and giving thanks amid the sound of a great celebration!
> —PSALM 42:4, NLT

In this verse I heard the cry of a man reminiscing about how good things used to be between himself and God. How in love he was with the Creator of the universe as he led worship for an entire nation, his heart overflowing with adoration for his God. Everything was right, and his life was perfect. Here he contrasts those good times with his current state of being, his heart begins to break, and he mourns the life he once had—the God he once knew.

I imagine him crying out to the God he could no longer feel: "God, I used to love You so much! We were so close—best friends! You were the sole object of my desire!"

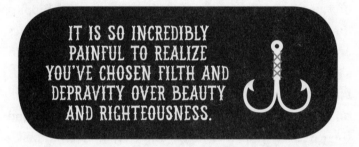

IT IS SO INCREDIBLY PAINFUL TO REALIZE YOU'VE CHOSEN FILTH AND DEPRAVITY OVER BEAUTY AND RIGHTEOUSNESS.

Pain is the only word capable of describing that kind of regret. It is so incredibly painful to realize you've chosen filth and depravity over beauty and righteousness. Your heart wrenches when you are coldly confronted with your reality and you see how distant it is from your destiny and God's promises for your life. Every good memory produces a deep, stabbing pain in your heart, matched only by the scorn from a former lover who promised to never leave again.

Peter writes in 2 Peter 2:20 that people who have known Jesus and then turned from Him are more miserable than if they had never known Him in the first place.

That was certainly true in my case. Life holds a different kind of misery for those who have known perfect love and then forsaken Him for futile pleasures. Maybe it was because I knew exactly what (whom) I'd turned from and given up on. Although I had become that scorning lover, somehow I ended up feeling all the pain in my heart.

MARKED BY ENCOUNTER

I had practically grown up in church, with pictures of this Jesus all around me. My parents were hippies, flower children of the sixties. They were both alcoholics and drug addicts, and their marriage was explosive, to say the least. Then in 1976 they were invited to a Jesus People home group meeting where the Holy Spirit fell on them. They gave their drugs, their depravity, and their lives to Jesus that night, and they went from being peace-loving hippies to radical Jesus Freaks.

My mother found out she was pregnant with me sometime after my parents became Christians. Shortly after I was born, my parents were ordained as pastors, and as a result I spent nearly every Sunday morning, Sunday night, and Wednesday night of my childhood in a pink church chair, staring at foam-green carpets. (It was the eighties, after all!)

Church had some really great moments, and Jesus became very real to me during my childhood. I had several powerful encounters with God that would come back to haunt me or sustain me as a prodigal. Not until much later did I learn that an encounter does not change your character; rather, it is meant to be an on-ramp for your choice to change. God will not use an encounter to violate your free will.

The sixth grade was a significant year for me in my relationship with the Holy Spirit. Every year I went to Bible camp in Devils Lake, North Dakota. (Yes, Devils Lake.) That year we had a speaker who quite literally changed my young life. His name was Reggie Dabbs, and he was and still is a powerhouse for Jesus and the kingdom of God. That summer, during his ministry, I received the gift of speaking in tongues, was slain in the Spirit for the first time, and experienced an open vision. Though no one touched me, it felt like a solid wave of water hit me and knocked me to the ground. Lying in the prayer room on the floor, for the first time ever I felt the tangible presence of the Lord. When I opened my eyes, I saw huge thunderclouds rip open and men coming through the clouds on horses. The face of the man leading the charge shined so brightly I could not actually see it. His whole face eclipsed the earth with brilliant light. I knew He was Jesus and the other men on horses were angels.

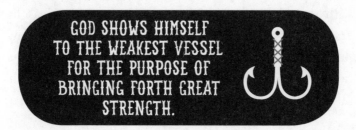

GOD SHOWS HIMSELF TO THE WEAKEST VESSEL FOR THE PURPOSE OF BRINGING FORTH GREAT STRENGTH.

As my vision continued, Jesus stepped His foot onto the earth, and everyone on the earth was cast into shadow in the presence of His brightness. At that moment, a city made of lights began to descend from heaven to the earth, and it was established as the City of God as Jesus began to remake the earth, bringing it back to its original form and purpose. Before I got up from the vision, Jesus spoke this to me: "I am the Lion of the tribe of Judah, and I will return."

I will never forget that vision. I realize now that I was "marked" that day, even though I did not have a deep relationship with Him. I was amazed Jesus would give me that kind of an encounter when I used filthy words and struggled sexually. And yet this is the nature of God—showing Himself to the weakest vessel for the purpose of bringing forth great strength.

GODLY SORROW

As a prodigal, I often thought I would never have any more happy memories. I completely wrote off ever having a house or a beautiful, sweet, faithful wife and children. I mourned the future I thought I had thrown away. As a result, all the memories of my encounters with Jesus left me embittered and calloused; I was literally haunted by them. Later I learned, "Godly sorrow produces repentance that leads to salvation and brings no regret, but the sorrow of the world produces death" (2 Cor. 7:10, MEV).

Godly sorrow produces mourning over sin, while worldly sorrow produces mourning over losses. It took a while before my sorrow turned from worldly to godly, resulting in my decision to repent and run back to Jesus. In the meantime all I could think about was poor old me and the life I could have had.

Still, in the midst of my self-centeredness, I would sometimes think about my Jesus encounters and wonder, *How could I have gotten this far?* It was like in the blink of an eye I went from being a preacher's kid who always fought for the little guy to being a drug addict begging to be loved or just be enough for other people. Somehow I had made the choice to allow Satan to distance me so far from home and my encounters with God that I felt I was beyond the point of return. So I did all I thought I could do: I mourned my losses rather than my sin. I mean, what was the point of repenting if God wouldn't take me back anyway, right?

See, once we completely lose sight of who God is and who He says we are, Satan proceeds to beat us with shame and hopelessness and tell us it's too little, too late.

But that's not God! *That's not God.*

Too often, people think God is the one telling them it's too late or they're too far from home. So they give up on even trying to come home; they stop repenting altogether. Layers of callousness build over their hearts, their ears deafen to the cries of the Holy Spirit, and they become so desensitized to sin that basically anything goes.

GODLY SORROW PRODUCES MOURNING OVER SIN, WHILE WORLDLY SORROW PRODUCES MOURNING OVER LOSSES.

The only voices that break through at that point are truth and love. The *truth* is that God never stops trying to find His lost sheep and bring them home; He doesn't give up. And *love* is that unconditional, unrelenting power that compelled a King to step off His throne and die the most horrific death in the history of humankind. When *truth* and *love* confront worldly sorrow with conviction, godly sorrow is produced, and repentance results.

CONVICTION VS. CONDEMNATION

As a prodigal, at times I could hear the Holy Spirit weeping over me. But never once did I hear Him say my sins had disqualified me. Even when I was breaking His heart, He wanted me and longed for me. Satan, on the other hand, never stopped accusing me.

This is the significant difference between the conviction of the Holy Spirit and the condemnation of Satan. Conviction is rooted in love; condemnation is rooted in shame. In Greek the word for conviction essentially means "proof of guilt," and the word for condemnation can be interpreted to mean no longer fit for use.[1] So while the Holy Spirit will show us the proof of our guilt to get us to repent, Satan will tell us we are no longer fit to be used by God to convince us to remain in our state of failure. The Holy Spirit's conviction is meant to mature us, while Satan's condemnation is meant to shame us and keep us immature. He wants to prevent us from fulfilling the destinies that have been placed in us and spoken over us.

When my mother found out she was pregnant with me, my parents already had two children and weren't planning on having any more. But there I was. My mother's favorite Bible story during that time was the story of Hannah and Samuel. Since my parents had not been planning to have another child, my mother decided to dedicate me to God's house forever, just as Samuel the prophet was.

I shudder when I think of how close Satan came to forever destroying the very destiny my mother spoke into me! He condemned me every chance he got, and he nearly succeeded at destroying me, because he convinced me to believe his lies about how God felt about me.

Many of us have very distorted beliefs about who God is, which makes it easy for Satan to convince us that God has given up on us and is out to condemn us. Satan speaks to us in the first person, in our thoughts, and because we are undiscerning, we perceive temptation as our own thoughts instead of seeing it for what it truly is—a lie. When we focus on our failures, we begin to believe lies about God and ourselves. Eventually Satan lies to us so much that we forget God has been longing, waiting, and watching for our homecoming. Satan expends all his energy deceiving and accusing God's children, while God is pleading and weeping for us to return because He so desperately wants to crown us with honor and victory, redemption and restoration.

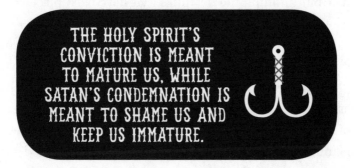

THE HOLY SPIRIT'S CONVICTION IS MEANT TO MATURE US, WHILE SATAN'S CONDEMNATION IS MEANT TO SHAME US AND KEEP US IMMATURE.

The good news is that it is never too late with God. While Satan may be in the business of destroying destinies, God is in the business of restoring destinies. God can (and wants to) restore all His lost children; He can (and He wants to!) restore you! He wants to give you back the joy of His salvation, which is what I like to describe as the joy you felt on the day you were saved. God doesn't want your memories to remain bittersweet; He doesn't want your destiny to remain unfulfilled. Allow Him to bring truth and love into your darkness and hopelessness. Allow Him to lead you home and bring you back to life by turning your worldly sorrow into godly sorrow.

You don't have to keep dwelling on those bittersweet memories, and you don't have to reminisce about how good things used to be. Let God redeem your years in a distant land. Turn away from your squalor, come home, and make new memories with your Jesus, who is so madly in love with you.

> In the same way, there is more joy in heaven over one lost sinner who repents and returns to God...
>
> —LUKE 15:7, NLT

We serve a God who wants to crawl into your pain with you, not isolate you when you're hurting.

Chapter 3

FOREFATHERS OF FAILURE

MOSES MAY HAVE HAD A STUTTERING PROBLEM, but I was certified learning disabled and ADHD. Seriously. I barely graduated high school with Ds, and I couldn't hold down a steady job. From third grade onward, I had to go to special classes with other disabled kids while my friends went to normal classes. It was humiliating to be labeled a special-needs kid, and I did everything I could to make sure no one knew. I would

hide my Ritalin from classmates, and I always made sure
to hide out in the bathrooms or lounge around until the
hallways were completely clear before making a mad
dash to my class for kids with special needs. Sometimes
I would even hide out in random classrooms, eliciting
confused stares from teachers and students.

It was hard for me to believe I would ever be used
for anything in God's kingdom. I certainly didn't believe
what people prophesied over me as a kid—that I would
be a prophetic voice and do great and wonderful things
for Jesus. Imagine how much harder this was to believe
once I became a prodigal and major screwup. But the
bigger surprise was that God did and is still doing these
things in me. In the same way, He holds on to the dignity and destiny of all prodigals, just waiting to crown
them again with the value they threw away.

Hudson Taylor, the great missionary to China, once
said, "All God's giants have been weak people."[1] It's not
that God has a sense of humor but that He loves to work in
paradoxes in order to confound the wisdom of the world.
Paul writes that God purposely seeks out the foolish and
the weak, those who wouldn't be considered wise, mighty,
or noble in the flesh, to shame the wise and strong things
of the world (1 Cor. 1:26–27). Jesus literally takes the
underdogs and makes Himself shine through them.

God demonstrated this in the life of Jesus. In the lineage of Jesus, in the beginning of the Book of Matthew,
we find out that Jesus had Gentiles in His bloodline as
well as a temple prostitute whose name literally means

"wide."[2] Think about the manger scene, which we love to romanticize. The cold, hard reality is that Jesus was born in an animal's toilet. God did not give Jesus a leg up in this story so that one day Jesus could give you one. He is the champion of the underdog.

JESUS LITERALLY TAKES THE UNDERDOGS AND MAKES HIMSELF SHINE THROUGH THEM.

We see God doing this throughout the Bible, especially in Hebrews 11, which is known as the Hall of Faith. It lists men and women considered by God to be hall-of-famers in faith. However, Hebrews 11 could have easily been turned into the Hall of Shame if any one of these great individuals had not gotten back up after they failed. In fact, many of these men and women had major character flaws. Many of the great men and women in the Bible were total screwups in the natural sense. Many were so questionable that few (if any) modern-day pastors would put them as heads of any ministry of any kind in their church.

Yet God came to these broken, messed-up people, and rather than condemn them or speak of their weaknesses, He called forth the destinies He had placed in them. Many of the men and women we see in the Bible were not good men and women because of the reality of their brokenness. But "God sees not as man sees, for man looks at the outward appearance, but the LORD looks at the heart" (1 Sam. 16:7, NAS).

NOAH

Two things are usually associated with Noah: the building of the ark, and his character as a man of great faith and steadfastness. Noah actually began as "a righteous man, the only blameless person living on earth at the time" (Gen. 6:9, NLT). He consistently followed God's will and enjoyed a close relationship with Him, so it's shocking that someone as righteous as Noah would later get drunk and naked and then curse his son's descendants in anger.

The only thing we're told in Genesis about Noah after he cursed his son is that he lived a couple hundred more years and then died at 950 years of age. What a sad ending, or so it seems! But the actual last time we hear about Noah in the Bible is in the New Testament—in Hebrews 11, 1 Peter, and 2 Peter. These three accounts make no mention of Noah's sin—not at all. Instead, God chose to only speak of Noah's faithfulness and righteousness. Even though humans would forever place an asterisk by Noah's name, God would not.

ABRAHAM AND SARAH

I used to always question Abraham and Sarah's place in the Hall of Faith. I actually considered them to be the poster children for what happens when you're not faithful. In addition to Abraham's fateful tryst with Hagar, Abraham was also a liar and coward who got so scared at one point that he nearly allowed his wife to be raped so his own life would be spared. Abraham was also a pagan moon-worshipper from Ur of the Chaldeans, the epicenter of moon worship during those times. He was such a faithful moon-worshipper that God may have seen his devotion and thought, "I want that for Myself."

Yet despite all of this, Hebrews 11 identifies and defines Abraham and Sarah in their redemptive state— as obedient, faithful worshippers who blindly trusted in God. God even chose to begin the lineage of His chosen people with Abraham and Sarah, in all their weaknesses, and He allowed Himself to be dubbed "the God of Abraham."

JACOB

Jacob stole his brother Esau's birthright; and if that wasn't enough, he also stole Esau's blessing by scheming with his mother to deceive his old, blind father, Isaac. No wonder Esau tried to kill him! Jacob escaped, and the next thing we know, he's wrestling with the angel of the Lord to get another blessing. (Most theologians believe the angel of the Lord was a theophany, or an appearance of Jesus in human form prior to His life on Earth.) In other words, Jacob actually strong-armed Jesus!

GOD CHOSE, BLESSED, AND LOVED ONE OF THE MOST DEVIOUS MEN IN THE BIBLE.

Rather than striking Jacob dead (as many of us would have done), God actually blessed him, changed his name to Israel, and made him the namesake for God's chosen people. The incredible thing is that God continued to refer to him as Jacob rather than using his new name. Hebrews 11:21 says, "By faith Jacob..." and Malachi 1:2–3 and Romans 9:13 say, "Jacob I have loved, but Esau I have hated" (MEV). God chose, blessed, and loved one of the most devious men in the Bible.

JOSEPH

Now *Joseph* was a spoiled brat. He knew he was his daddy's favorite, and he acted like it. People often look at Joseph like he was a poor, sweet boy who got bullied by his older brothers. But Joseph had a ton of pride issues, and he was also a little tattletale. For a while Joseph was all about "me, me, me."

We don't see Joseph as a truly humble man until he's standing before Pharaoh. Then, after his brothers come to him, starving and pitiful, Joseph plays a mean-spirited game with them that nearly sends Israel to his grave. Even despite all Joseph's selfishness, pride, and bitterness, God's hand was on him, and he was made second-in-command to Pharaoh, the most powerful man in the world at that time. Through Joseph, millions were saved from starvation. Hebrews 11 calls Joseph faithful, and his story in Genesis ends with him prophesying the Israelites' great deliverance.

MOSES

Moses was a smart, very well-educated man who grew up filthy rich as the adopted grandson of the pharaoh. He was what we'd consider a "trust fund baby" today, even despite his stuttering problem. He also had major anger issues, which caused him to murder a man (and later prevented him from entering the Promised Land). But what God saw was Moses's heart for His people. God called Moses His friend and considered Moses the most humble man alive.

This was after God found Moses while he was exiled in Midian. By then he was a lonesome, nearly eighty-year-old shepherd who had given up on ever doing anything significant with his life. Not only did God use Moses to deliver the Israelites, who had been enslaved for four hundred years, but He also picked Moses as the only living man who came face-to-face with the uncreated God of the universe.

DAVID

David was a rapist and a murderer. As king, he decided he wanted to sleep with a married woman, so he sent messengers "and took her" (2 Sam. 11:4). According to Nathan the prophet's parallel account in 2 Samuel 12, Bathsheba was an innocent lamb forcibly taken, not a willing participant. After David raped and impregnated her, he tried to cover up his transgression by having her husband murdered. These heinous acts overshadow every great thing David did—at least for us.

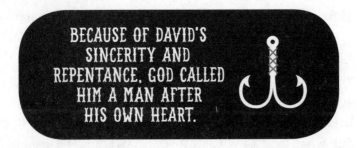

BECAUSE OF DAVID'S SINCERITY AND REPENTANCE, GOD CALLED HIM A MAN AFTER HIS OWN HEART.

But God doesn't think like us. He knew that while David did some vile things, he never repeated the same sin. It was because of his sincerity and repentance that God called David a man after His own heart (Acts 13:22). David alone received the honor of being called this by God. God also did something I always found shocking— yet so illustrative of His kindness. He took David's child to Bathsheba (not the first child, who died, but the second one), who must have been a constant reminder to David of his sin, and God chose that child as the next king.

RAHAB

Rahab is one of only two women mentioned in the Hall of Faith, and it's no secret she was a prostitute. In fact,

Hebrews 11 identifies her as "the prostitute Rahab" (Heb. 11:31, MEV). Rahab's name literally means "wide," in reference to her legs. Needless to say, Rahab did not always live a righteous life, yet God singled her out among an entire nation of Canaanites. Here was a woman probably despised by her own family and mocked and scorned everywhere she went. But when God scanned Jericho looking for someone to be part of His beautiful, epic story, Rahab the prostitute caught His eye.

"There," He said, His eyes filled with love and compassion, "I choose her." And in one fell swoop, God crowned her with honor and used her to shield His spies and save her family. Then God took it a step further. He told Joshua to let Rahab and her relatives live among the Israelites and to essentially become part of God's chosen people. But that wasn't enough. No, God wanted more for Rahab. So He gave her a husband, then He gave her an honorable son named Boaz, and hundreds of years later, He gave her a perfect great-grandson named Jesus.

GIDEON AND SAMSON

Hebrews 11 also counts Gideon and Samson among the faithful. Remember Gideon, whom God called "a mighty man of valor" while he was hiding out in a barn? And Samson, the Nazarene, whose lust for a pagan woman got him blinded and cost him his life? The Bible not only calls the men and women in Hebrews 11 faithful, but it says the world was not worthy of them. Even though they had so many character issues, God considered them champions of the faith. *Wow.*

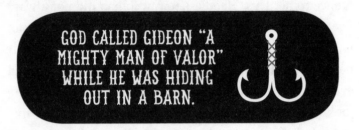

GOD CALLED GIDEON "A MIGHTY MAN OF VALOR" WHILE HE WAS HIDING OUT IN A BARN.

But God's faithfulness to those who'd failed didn't end in the Old Testament.

Chapter 4

FILTHY FISHERMEN

WE SEE IN THE NEW TESTAMENT THAT JESUS treated people with this same kindness and mercy. After all, He is the same "yesterday, and today, and forever" (Heb. 13:8, MEV).

The disciples Jesus chose were those who had been passed by in life. In those days rabbis would walk up to young boys of promise and say, "Follow me." This was one of the highest honors, because it meant that young man would be a rabbi. But if he was older than twelve, it wasn't going to happen.[1]

The fishermen in Jesus's day were rough, rugged, unchurched men. Tax collectors were even worse—Jews who profited from the Roman Empire's oppression of their own people. These men were greedy and often demanded overpayment of taxes, which they used to line their own pockets. Yet Jesus said to these filthy fishermen and ruthless tax collectors, "Follow Me." They were unwanted by the traditional religious infrastructure, but Jesus saw value in them. He wanted them for Himself.

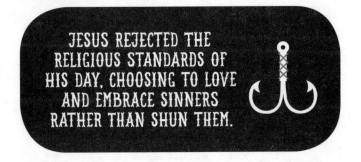

JESUS REJECTED THE RELIGIOUS STANDARDS OF HIS DAY, CHOOSING TO LOVE AND EMBRACE SINNERS RATHER THAN SHUN THEM.

Jesus was a bit of a renegade. He rejected the religious standards of His day, choosing to love and embrace sinners rather than shun them. He picked outcasts to be in His inner circle, and He chose to dine with "notorious sinners." Take this story for example:

> Later, Levi invited Jesus and his disciples to his home as dinner guests, along with many tax collectors and other disreputable sinners. (There were many people of this kind among Jesus' followers.) But when the teachers of religious law

who were Pharisees saw him eating with tax collectors and other sinners, they asked his disciples, "Why does he eat with such scum?"
—MARK 2:15–16, NLT

Jesus responded to these religious stoics, "Those who are well have no need of a physician, but those who are sick. I came not to call the righteous, but sinners to repentance" (Mark 2:17, MEV). The word *well*, which is used in some translations of that verse, in the Greek means "to have power as shown by extraordinary deeds," or the ability to overcome in your own strength.[2] The word *sick* in the Greek can be interpreted to mean to have grief and cause grief.[3] Jesus knew the weaknesses of these sinners, but He chose to make Himself vulnerable to them, to give them a chance at transformation by exposing them to perfect love. Though some would indeed be transformed, others would not. Still, Jesus was relentless in loving them, and He never thought twice about making Himself available to them.

PETER

Peter was one of the three disciples closest to Jesus. An arrogant, rambunctious fisherman, he was always trying to prove himself to everyone around him. But during a critical hour, Peter was able to look at his best friend—beaten, beard ripped out, drenched in blood—and say, "I don't know Him." On his third denial, the Bible tells us Peter cursed (Matt. 26:74).

Jesus wasn't surprised by Peter's denial; He had predicted it. In fact, Jesus had declared He would build His church upon Peter while knowing Peter would vehemently deny Him (Matt. 16:18). The knowledge of Peter's future failure did not deter Jesus's affection for Peter. In fact, Jesus prayed for Peter, knowing this would happen. During the Last Supper, Jesus turned to Peter and said:

> Simon, Simon, Satan has asked to sift each of you like wheat. But I have pleaded in prayer for you, Simon, that your faith should not fail. So when you have repented and turned to me again, strengthen your brothers.
>
> —LUKE 22:31–32, NLT

Not surprisingly, Peter was very ashamed of himself after he denied Jesus. Peter evidently forgot what Jesus had told him at the Last Supper, and he basically gave up and went back to his old career, fishing. However, after His resurrection, Jesus tracked Peter down in order to address this heavy shame and remind him of His words.

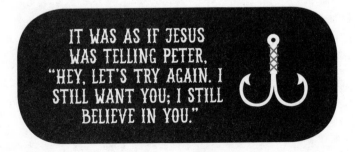

IT WAS AS IF JESUS WAS TELLING PETER, "HEY, LET'S TRY AGAIN. I STILL WANT YOU; I STILL BELIEVE IN YOU."

Early one morning after His resurrection, Jesus made Peter breakfast and then asked him three consecutive times: "Peter, do you love Me?" (See John 21:15–17.) Each time, Peter responded, "Yes, Lord, You know that I love You." On the third time, the Bible says, "Peter was hurt that Jesus asked the question a third time" (John 21:17, NLT). Peter didn't realize what Jesus was doing. With each declaration, Jesus broke the shame off Peter's heart caused by his three denials. Peter needed to know that he did in fact love Jesus, despite his denial. And after Jesus restored Peter, He told him, "Follow Me"—just like He did on their first encounter (John 21:19). It was as if Jesus was telling Peter, "Hey, let's try again. I still want you; I still believe in you." I believe this encounter so transformed and ignited Peter that his first sermon resulted in three thousand salvations (Acts 2:41).

JAMES AND JOHN

These brothers were nicknamed "the Sons of Thunder" because they had so much zeal. While they were with Jesus, they were immature, selfish, and egotistical. John was also an elitist who tried to stop someone from using Jesus's name to cast out a demon because that person wasn't part of their group (Luke 9:49). James and John also once asked Jesus to "call down fire from heaven" to burn up Samaritans who rejected their group, which earned them a rebuke from Jesus (Luke 9:54–55, NLT).

The Gospel of Mark also tells us their egos began to cause dissension in the group, forcing Jesus to intervene (Mark 10:35–41). Immediately after Jesus told His disciples He was going to be betrayed, mocked, spit on, beaten, and killed, James and John asked Him to do them a favor and allow them to sit on His immediate left and right in heaven. Matthew 20:20 tells us it was their mother who asked for this favor. This argument about who would be greatest arose again right after Jesus told them the grievous news that one of the disciples would betray Him (Luke 22:21–24).

Yet James and John were two of the three disciples (along with Peter) who comprised Jesus's innermost circle. Even with all their issues and insensitivities, Jesus trusted them and allowed them to accompany Him for His most powerful miracles and most intimate prayer trips. Jesus may have known their present weaknesses, but He chose to define them by His eternal knowledge of them.

James would later become the first Christian martyr, beheaded for his faith. John, however, would outlive all the other disciples to become a mentor to many in the early church. God took John's immaturity and selfish ambition and held it under the radiation therapy of perfect love until John was so transformed that he refused to be defined by anything other than the title "the disciple whom Jesus loved." He wrote the Gospel of John, where he humbly laid out all his sins and weaknesses for the world to see. He also wrote the first, second, and third Epistles of John, and while banished to Patmos at ninety-two years of age—after surviving being dunked in boiling oil—John received a radical vision and wrote the final book of the Bible, the Revelation of Jesus Christ.

JUDAS ISCARIOT

Judas Iscariot must also be included in this list of filthy fishermen. After all, in Jesus's treatment of Judas Iscariot we get a true glimpse into Jesus's heart toward the sinner. How does Jesus treat the person He knows will sell Him out to be murdered? And an even greater question is, how would *you* treat a Judas?

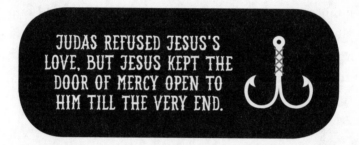

JUDAS REFUSED JESUS'S LOVE, BUT JESUS KEPT THE DOOR OF MERCY OPEN TO HIM TILL THE VERY END.

Jesus made Himself safe enough for Judas. After choosing His disciples, Jesus said, "I chose the twelve of you, but one is a devil" (John 6:70, NLT). Jesus allowed Judas to be in His inner circle and even allowed Judas to be the disciples' treasurer, knowing he was a disloyal thief. Every day for the next three years, Jesus gave Judas opportunities to confess the sins of his heart and repent. Jesus even washed Judas's feet, hoping this ultimate act of humility toward a sinner would lead him to repentance. But Judas refused Jesus's love. Still, Jesus kept the door of mercy open to Judas till the very end. "In great anguish of spirit," Jesus finally revealed that it would be one of His disciples, one of His best friends, who would betray Him (John 13:21, TLB).

Jesus took zero pleasure in revealing His betrayer—it absolutely devastated Him. David had prophesied hundreds of years earlier, "Even my best friend, the one I trusted completely, the one who shared my food, has turned against me" (Ps. 41:9, NLT). Thus, with pleading eyes, knowing the fate that awaited Judas, Jesus handed him bread as if to tell him he had one more opportunity to repent. Instead, Judas coolly ate the bread, and in that moment, "Satan entered into him. Then Jesus told him 'Hurry and do what you're going to do'" (John 13:27–28, NLT). In the story of Judas Iscariot, we see God's patience, "not wanting anyone to perish, but everyone to come to repentance" (2 Pet. 3:9, NIV). This applies to everyone— even a thief and a traitor like Judas Iscariot.

SAUL OF TARSUS

Saul's transformation into Paul is another vivid demonstration of God's mercy. Before he became Paul the Apostle, Saul of Tarsus was the worst among sinners (1 Tim. 1:15). The Bible tells us Saul not only held the coats of the Pharisees when they fatally stoned Stephen, a deacon of the early church, but he also "agreed completely with the killing of Stephen" (Acts 8:1, NLT). He became a key figure in the massive wave of persecution that came against the early church, going everywhere to drag Christians out of their homes and imprison them (Acts 8:3). In the verses immediately preceding his fateful encounter with Jesus, Saul was "uttering threats with every breath and was eager to kill the Lord's followers" (Acts 9:1, NLT).

It was as if God looked down from heaven, saw Saul's zeal, and decided He would channel it for Himself. And God would use everything—Paul's background, training, citizenship, and even weaknesses—for His glory. When Ananias protested having to pray for Saul, God told him:

> Go [and do what I say], for Saul is my chosen instrument to take my message to the Gentiles and to kings, as well as to the people of Israel. And I will show him how much he must suffer for my name's sake.
>
> —ACTS 9:15–16, NLT

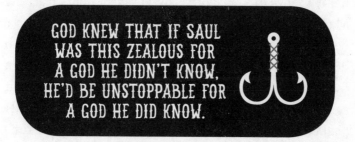

GOD KNEW THAT IF SAUL WAS THIS ZEALOUS FOR A GOD HE DIDN'T KNOW, HE'D BE UNSTOPPABLE FOR A GOD HE DID KNOW.

God knew that if Saul was this zealous for a God he didn't know, he'd be unstoppable for a God he did know. So an encounter with Jesus in the middle of the road, coupled with a single miracle, turned a Jesus-hating Saul into a Bible-writing Paul. Indeed, God radically used Paul to write thirteen of the twenty-seven books in the New Testament. And Paul, who used to kill Christians, was beaten, tortured, imprisoned, and eventually beheaded because he was a Christian.

WOMEN

In Jesus's day being a woman was a definite disadvantage. Yet Jesus treated women with radical kindness and gave them value in a culture that had no value for them. Back then, women were incredibly oppressed and regarded as nothing more than property; they had the social status of slaves and were prohibited from speaking in public. In fact, it was near criminal for men to speak to women in public, and Jewish tradition forbade the teaching of women.

Yet women were among Jesus's most devoted followers. He defended the adulteress and then empowered her with love to live righteously. He spent hours teaching Mary Magdalene, even setting her free from multiple demonic spirits. And He also sought out a woman so desperate to find love that she had tried and failed in five different marriages. She was an outcast among outcasts who was so misunderstood and scorned by her peers that she went to get water during the hottest time of the day, when everyone else stayed indoors, in order to avoid their whispers and judgmental glares. But when He found her, Jesus loved her, restored her broken heart, accepted her, and then used her to lead many of her fellow Samaritans to Him.

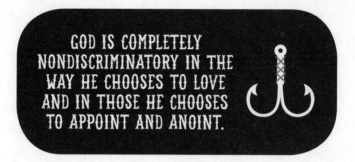

GOD IS COMPLETELY NONDISCRIMINATORY IN THE WAY HE CHOOSES TO LOVE AND IN THOSE HE CHOOSES TO APPOINT AND ANOINT.

Though society had labeled women as worthless, Jesus found them to be valuable and worthy of His time and attention. Jesus was the original women's rights activist, and He challenged the oppressive culture of His day.

In these many examples of "filthy fishermen," we see that God is completely nondiscriminatory in the way He chooses to love and in those He chooses to appoint and anoint. He loves the weak, the strong, and the oppressed all alike. Both the sinner and the saint. As we read through the Bible, it seems as if God purposely sought out screwups—maybe because He saw them as the greatest opportunities for redemption. And Judas Iscariot is an example of an everyday reality: Jesus makes Himself available to even the most wicked of sinners and loves them unconditionally, so that when (or if) they choose to turn to Him, He is ready with a crown of honor and redemption.

Where Satan tries to create screwups, God goes on a mission to redeem them.

Chapter 5

LOVE SONGS
FOR HARLOTS

A S ONE SUCH SCREWUP, I SPENT SEVEN YEARS running from God. But my rebellion actually started three years earlier, when I was seventeen.

At the beginning of my junior year in high school, I had an amazing motley crew of friends, and I was dating a girl I was madly in love with. I went to church and played "Christian music" with my punk rock band, but I had begun to slowly turn my back on God by occasionally drinking and getting high. Soon, I became convinced God no longer liked me, but I was too ashamed to confess my struggles and doubts. I was also hoping to fool my parents. (They say it didn't work.)

What had started out as a seemingly great year quickly became a nightmare when one of my friends suddenly died from complications from the flu. It devastated our small community and terrorized me. I began having vivid nightmares in which my friend would visit me from the grave. I would wake up sobbing, feeling very angry with God for not protecting me from those bad dreams. I didn't realize that when you make agreements with darkness, you take away God's legal right to step in and help. In other words, God would not violate my free will. Since by my own free will I had taken areas of my life and handed them over to Satan (through drinking and getting high), I had tied God's hands, so to speak. I'm not saying we are stronger than God, but He has promised by His own great name not to violate the order He created, including human free will. God will not contradict Himself.

GOD WILL NOT VIOLATE
OUR FREE WILL.

My friend's death was the first offense that sank deeply into my heart and attacked my faith. I couldn't believe God would kill my friend like that; it seemed so incredibly unfair and unjust. I thought, "Why couldn't You kill someone who was evil? Why did You kill one of my best friends?" In my thinking at that time, it made sense to me that God was responsible for all death. (It's amazing what you can accuse Him of when you don't really know Him!)

During this period of grieving, my girlfriend went missing for nine days with my car. I was so worried about her that I couldn't eat or sleep. Then one afternoon my parents' kitchen phone rang, and it was her! My cheeks flushed and my heart began to pound. "Are you OK? What happened to you? Do you need help?" I asked.

To my relief, she was fine. But the next words out of her mouth shattered me: she told me she had found someone else she wanted to be with. My knees buckled beneath me, my stomach curled, and my mind raced. I felt like someone had driven a two-by-four right through my chest. It literally took the breath out of me. I loved this girl deeper than I was aware of until that moment. My father caught me as I collapsed onto the kitchen floor, heaving and sobbing. I had lost a good friend, and now I had lost the first girl I had ever truly loved.

GIVING UP

Time went on, and I began to heal slowly, even though I was still distant from God. My parents saw the way I was falling from grace, and while they confronted me, they didn't push. They watched as I began to slip farther and farther from God. One night my father invited me to church because a prophetic minister from Canada was coming. At the service the minister called me out and spoke the heart of God over me. I was so encouraged and hopeful that I went home that night and played Bible roulette. I grabbed my Bible from under my bed, opened it, and with my eyes closed, pointed to a random place, hoping God would give me a verse.

I landed in Hosea 1:1. (I didn't even know Hosea was a book in the Bible.) I started to read, thinking, "OK, God, I'm going to give You another shot here," as if I was a star player God really needed on His team.

I enjoyed the drama of God telling Hosea to marry a prostitute named Gomer, and I read that Gomer cheated on Hosea with other men and actually had children with other men while she was married to Hosea. I had just gone through the trauma of being dumped by my girlfriend for another guy, so I was very excited to be reading this in a book from the Old Testament. I thought this was where it was going to get good! I couldn't wait for God to send down fire and burn Gomer up for what she had done! However, that was not what happened; Gomer did not get punished. Instead, after Gomer cheated on Hosea, God told Hosea to go and buy her back.

This was a reality I was too wounded to understand or accept, since I wasn't yet healed from my own wound of betrayal. I became angry and offended at God. "Either

You're a pervert or You're powerless," I accused Him, "and I am not interested in either."

I gave up on God that day. I walked away, deciding my life was miserable because I'd been trying so hard to please my family, church people, and Him. My whole life I had been labeled as someone with special learning needs, and as a result I had incredibly low self-esteem. On top of that, I had been hurt by family, I had lost friends, and I had lost the girl I thought I was going to marry. The enemy used all of this to convince me that God could not and would not help me, and that even if He did, it would not be worth much. Although I wouldn't blaspheme God, I resolved to quit caring. And so began my dark, seven-year journey of running from and openly rebelling against God.

After high school, I was still living in Minot, North Dakota, but I decided it was time to move out of my parents' house. I got a job at Taco Bell. In 1997, whoever was running that Taco Bell on North Hill in Minot hired all punk rockers. I was the guy behind the counter with a big red Mohawk, black eyeliner, black lipstick, black fingernail polish, and a big smile. My coworkers and I looked like a bunch of out-of-work circus clowns, but we thought we were awesome. People would walk into the lobby, see us, turn around, and leave.

ALTHOUGH I WOULDN'T BLASPHEME GOD, I RESOLVED TO QUIT CARING.

So there I was, living on my own in a tiny efficiency apartment, playing in a punk rock band and slinging tacos to pay the rent. One day, a Colombian gentleman walked into my Taco Bell and approached me about a "job opportunity." I happily accepted his offer, excited to do anything other than make tacos. Without going into all the details, I will say that my time working for this gentleman became one of the darkest times in my life. Still, the grace of God anchored me and protected me when I didn't deserve it.

During that time I also began to fall hard for a lesbian in my social scene. She confessed that she, too, had a crush on me. This was a huge compliment to me because I had incredibly low self-esteem, and this girl who wasn't supposed to like me was enamored with me. She moved in with me, and I really thought I was in love. I gave so much of myself away to this girl. My whole life, I had been chasing love, just wanting to be enough for somebody. I just wanted a girl who was sweet and would love me for who I was. I was tired of dating mean girls or girls who were more jacked up than I was. At the end of our relationship, I discovered that this girl had been cheating on me with a woman, as well as lying to all my close friends about our relationship.

I was a wreck. I went on a heavy drinking binge, but the grace of God intervened again, and I managed to call my father one night. I told him, "If you don't come get me, I'm not going to make it through the night." Within hours, my father came and got me. The next day, he got me out of my lease and onto a train to Marion, Ohio, to stay with my sister and her husband.

Every night for the next three weeks, this girl called me, crying and saying she never meant to cheat on me. She begged me to come back and promised everything would be OK. Sadly I had made a significant soul tie with this girl, and I could not resist. I asked one of my best friends for money for a train ticket, and as soon as I got it, I hopped on that train back to Minot, North Dakota—back to my Egypt.

I sat on the train, smoking pack after pack of cigarettes and looking at the countryside as I rocketed back home to her and what I hoped was another shot at love. When I got off the train, I combed the crowds, searching wildly for her. For two hours I searched and waited, but she never came. So I took my luggage and walked to her apartment, hoping she had just written down the wrong time. When I got there, I found her sitting and holding hands with the woman she had left me for.

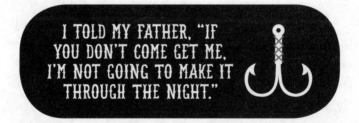

I TOLD MY FATHER, "IF YOU DON'T COME GET ME, I'M NOT GOING TO MAKE IT THROUGH THE NIGHT."

"You weren't supposed to be here yet," was all she said.

My heart dropped into my stomach, and I walked out. I couldn't bring myself to move back in with my parents, so I again called my best friend. His family was Christian in the truest, nonreligious, and most relational sense of the word. They let me move in and live with them for six months, allowed me to eat all their food, and loved me even when I broke stuff in their house and made a mess. They were a lighthouse for me. They were the real deal.

Eventually I moved out and found myself living in Fargo, North Dakota, playing in a punk rock band and working at a record store that sold drug paraphernalia in the back. I started abusing painkillers, taking up to two hundred Vicodin per week to numb the pain of loneliness, disappointment, shame, and a million other emotions. The pills also made it much easier to be around my friends or family, because I always felt shame when I looked at them. Prodigals have a thing with not wanting to be seen by their loved ones, and they feel the same way toward God. I guess it's because they don't want their loved ones or God to see how disappointing they are.

My parents would call to check on me and tell me they loved me, and I would lie and tell them I was OK—along with other things I thought they wanted to hear. I wanted to make them proud, to be good enough for them, and to erase the tone of disappointment and frustration in their voices. But they knew the truth, and love wouldn't allow them to give up.

DIVINE ENCOUNTER

I quickly became lonely and even more depressed living in Fargo, as I wrestled with feelings of worthlessness and isolation. One day, I lost my job at the record store, and I became very desperate to be around people. I decided I would not kill myself if I went to the mall to be around people. Here is proof God really has a way of orchestrating events. As I walked through the mall, depressed and high on Vicodin, I heard someone calling my name. This struck fear in my heart. I hated running into Christians, because they were either very mean or very emotional toward me. I was shocked anyone knew me and was even more shocked when I saw the person the voice belonged to—the nurse from the youth Bible camp I had attended as a teenager! She had always been so kind to me, no matter what color my hair was or what new tattoo I was showing off at camp. She didn't even live in Fargo, but she told me she had been trying to find me and was just passing through Fargo when she decided to go to the mall. This is what we call a divine encounter.

Turns out she had been having dreams about me standing and ministering to thousands of people. My words were like arrows to the hearts of the people, and I was changing lives and changing environments. She said golden arrows were coming out of my mouth and piercing the hearts of people.

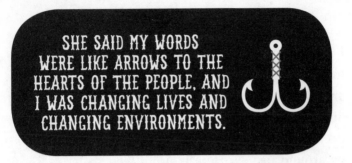

SHE SAID MY WORDS
WERE LIKE ARROWS TO THE
HEARTS OF THE PEOPLE, AND
I WAS CHANGING LIVES AND
CHANGING ENVIRONMENTS.

It was really exciting stuff to hear—unless you were like me and had been receiving prophetic words your whole life. Theoretically it might sound nice to hear words of hope when you're hopeless, but when you don't believe you deserve kind words, they simply serve as a stinging reminder of what you've wasted. By that point, I knew all I had to do as a prodigal to repel Christians was to yell at them—so I yelled at her.

"And how am I supposed to get there? Look at me! I'm a drug addict!"

Instead of running away, she spoke with confidence right back at me, saying, "Find an old friend and get mentored!" She frightened me; I wasn't used to Christians yelling back at me. I decided to give it a shot and went looking for a church.

Surprisingly the youth pastor at the church I chose was a counselor at the same Bible camp the nurse had worked at. I decided to confess everything to him. I told him, "I'm addicted to drugs, my relationships are inappropriate, I'm addicted to porn, I hardly talk to my family, and I really miss God. I really need help. Can you help me?"

He responded by inviting me to an all-night pizza party the following week. I explained that I was twenty-five years old and didn't want to do those things. After I pressed him to pray right then, he offered up a two-second prayer and told me to make an appointment for the next week to receive more prayer. I called him for weeks with no response and finally realized he was blowing me off. I felt burned and hurt by the church once again. So I walked away from God, telling Him the church was a poor choice for a people since they were critical, only interested in themselves, and didn't love others. I was through with them.

Little did I know, I was headed toward an encounter with Jesus—the Man named *grace.*

Chapter 6

OFFENSIVE GRACE

HERE'S THE THING ABOUT GRACE. IT IS ALWAYS sufficient, always enough for what we need. And like Jesus, it is sometimes very offensive. As a prodigal I know that, because I've lived it. I've met the man named grace, and I've seen what He can do.

Conceptually grace is difficult to understand simply because it is an attribute of an infinite God. Our finite minds just cannot comprehend the fullness of who He is, and grace is one of the biggest mysteries. It goes farther than our taboos and takes us places our hang-ups can't go.

True grace offends us by lavishing itself upon someone we think (in our black-and-white world) deserves zero. This was my story. For me, grace was made perfect in the gray area, in serendipitous acts of God on my behalf that were totally undeserved. During my prodigal years, this grace acted as an anchor and protected me.

I attempt to define grace as just what you need at the right time to choose the right thing. But as Judas Iscariot illustrates, some people will still choose the wrong thing, even when presented with the purest form of grace—Jesus Himself. But that's the beauty of grace— God extends it to us, knowing we might not choose Him. Grace is so completely undeserved that it's not even based on God's omniscience. The power behind godly grace is that it keeps presenting us with opportunities to choose the right thing. As a result, I have almost never seen godly grace produce poor character; it has an anointing, and as a result, it produces fruit— even if that fruit shows up later than expected. Ungodly grace, on the other hand, is void of anointing and produces entitlement and exceptions for sin.

CAN'T BUY ME GRACE

To receive this free gift of grace, we need the anointing, the ability of the Spirit. We cannot receive it on our own. This is the beauty of grace. When Jesus called His disciples, He commissioned them to three great purposes that were unprecedented at that time: to operate in supernatural ministry, to freely receive the anointing for ministry, and to freely give it to others (Matt. 10:8). By contrast, the poison of the religious spirit causes us to be driven by an obligation to earn rewards from God. This is so far from God's heart of grace. So often, our true theology—what we really believe about God and grace—comes out of our private moments with God in how we live our lives and how we treat others, especially the undeserving.

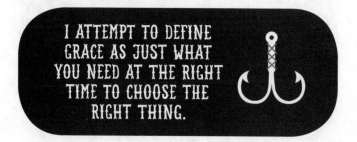

I ATTEMPT TO DEFINE GRACE AS JUST WHAT YOU NEED AT THE RIGHT TIME TO CHOOSE THE RIGHT THING.

Grace especially offends the religious person because it doesn't make any sense. Religion is based on the law and, as a result, works. By contrast, grace is based on Jesus's act of bearing the sins of the world on the cross. Paul wrote in Romans that the Jews, the pious religious folks, had a very difficult time understanding grace because they were so used to having to work for their salvation.

> I know what enthusiasm they have for God, but it is misdirected zeal. For they don't understand God's way of making people right with himself. Refusing to accept God's way, they cling to their own way of getting right with God by trying to keep the law.
> —Romans 10:2–3, nlt

Phrases like "saved by grace" didn't make sense to the Jews, which explains why they also had such a hard time understanding why Jesus would want to hang out with sinners. As Paul wrote, they didn't understand "God's way of making people right with himself." God's way is Jesus; the human way is works. God's way is a gift; the human way is a heavy yoke that breeds a religious spirit.

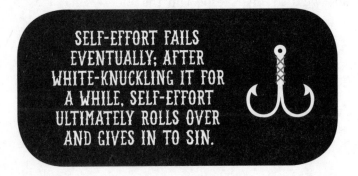

SELF-EFFORT FAILS EVENTUALLY; AFTER WHITE-KNUCKLING IT FOR A WHILE, SELF-EFFORT ULTIMATELY ROLLS OVER AND GIVES IN TO SIN.

People with religious mind-sets have a very difficult time really understanding that we cannot do *anything* to obtain grace. Grace is a wild card. But when we need it to make the right decision, it's there, because the grace of God is always sufficient. Grace, I believe, gets its strength from being captivated by Jesus. Those who are slaves to the law get their strength from self-effort. The problem with self-effort is that it fails eventually; after white-knuckling it for a while, self-effort ultimately rolls over and gives in to sin. However, grace empowered by captivation with Jesus holds steady, even when no one is around to watch.

GRACE THE GIFT

Often we struggle to understand grace because our concept of grace is based on works—on what we have earned or what we deserve. The problem is, true grace is not based on works at all. In grace, we get what we don't deserve; it is unobtainable. In other words, we cannot do anything to obtain it. If we have done something to earn grace, it's not true grace, because true grace is completely undeserved.

Paul is explicit in his description of grace: "For by grace you have been saved through faith. And this is not your own doing; it is the gift of God, not a result of works, so that no one may boast" (Eph. 2:8–9). Here Paul says grace is a gift from God that no one has done anything to earn so that no one can boast about anything he or she did. True grace brings glory to God, not people. Thus, it is a gift that can't be merited—only received.

As Christians, we don't have a problem with being "saved by grace," but many of us tend to have a problem with anything else by grace—like people being radically redeemed, restored, or made whole by grace. The Pharisee in us is troubled and offended by grace because it doesn't look like what we think is just or fair. Thus, when people sin—especially "major" sin—we think these people need a sort of "purgatory period" during which they must do something to prove themselves and earn back God's love (or even their salvation). Such ideas are *completely* contrary to biblical, godly grace. Jesus didn't demand purgatory. Instead, He told the thief hanging on the cross next to Him, "*Today* you will be with Me in Paradise" (Luke 23:43, MEV, emphasis added).

CALLING FOUL

Charles Spurgeon once said, "God is often exceedingly good to those who are utterly unworthy of such treatment."[1] I often think about revival when I think about grace. The two are closely connected. Revival doesn't look like a "good" church service when the worship team plays something in a minor key and the most current and relevant speaker delivers a stunning message. Nope. Revival looks like the crack whore who works the area near your church getting saved and delivered. Then, when she comes to your church and prays for someone in a wheelchair and that person is healed, you don't become offended that God didn't pick you to do the miracle, but you rejoice in God's goodness and grace for all.

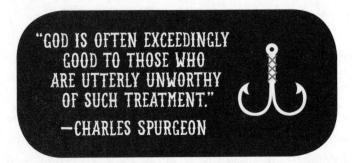

"GOD IS OFTEN EXCEEDINGLY GOOD TO THOSE WHO ARE UTTERLY UNWORTHY OF SUCH TREATMENT."
—CHARLES SPURGEON

That's real revival—a revival of grace. But when we witness God's goodness to unworthy people while we have unresolved wounds or religious mind-sets, we can become offended at God and turn from Him the way I did after reading the story of Hosea and Gomer.

Even now, years since I've been completely healed of those wounds, I still find the story of Hosea and Gomer incredibly offensive. First, God told Hosea, a prophet, to purchase a prostitute and marry her. God didn't force Hosea to love her, since God doesn't violate our free will. Instead, Hosea actually fell in love with Gomer. He even had kids with her. Then, sure enough, Gomer went sneaking around behind Hosea's back and ended up having multiple kids with multiple men. But instead of telling him to kick her to the curb or stone her to death, God told Hosea to buy Gomer back and even take on her illegitimate kids as his own!

It's one of those stories where—if you personally knew Hosea—you'd think he was crazy for not ditching Gomer. If he was your friend, you'd try to talk him out of letting her come home. And when he didn't listen, you'd probably get angry and disgusted with him. It might even ruin your friendship. Yet this ugly picture is a portrait of God's grace, His extreme goodness to those who are totally undeserving.

When I was deep in sin, I could still hear God. How is that possible? Incredibly, God never removes the gifts or callings He has placed in us, no matter how badly we mess up or divert from our God-given destinies. As Romans 11:29 says, "For the gifts and calling of God are irrevocable" (MEV). God doesn't take away His gift, but

He removes His anointing. It is part of His grace and goodness toward the undeserving.

I was called to be a prophet from birth; it was the calling God placed on me. Though God withheld His anointing during those years, He did not remove His gifting, and I could still hear Him. In fact, I would even use the things He told me to pick up girls in bars or freak out my friends at parties. I had a gift, but it was anointed by something other than God. It's not something I'm proud of, but it definitely illustrates the irrevocability of God's gifts and the extent of His grace and goodness toward prodigals.

THE KINDNESS OF JESUS

Many of us have been taught that when we do something bad, God punishes us. However, the truth is, God is not interested in punishing us. Where the Bible says He chastises those He loves in Hebrews 12:6, the word for *chastises* in the Greek can be interpreted to mean to bring to maturity through teaching.[2] It doesn't mean He punishes those He loves. God's primary tool for leading people back to Him is His goodness. Paul writes that it is the goodness of God, His kindness, that leads people to repentance (Rom. 2:4). The grace of God is also kindness. And it was this grace, in the form of Jesus's kindness, that ended my seven-year prodigal run.

After I had a heart attack and fell off the stage, after Wendy the stripper/witch took me to the roof of the music venue for an hour and a half and then to the hospital, where she left me sobbing and alone, Jesus literally appeared to me. As I sobbed in my bed, feeling utterly hopeless and alone, suddenly Jesus came into my room through the ceiling. Tranquility (and bewilderment) instantly displaced my hopelessness, and in that moment, I was overwhelmed by His kindness.

Ever so gently, Jesus put His hand on my head at the same place where Wendy had touched me while offering up "good prayers" for me. Then He softly said, "Hello."

Somehow I managed to blurt out a weak, "Hi."

"You fought so hard," Jesus said to me in the gentlest, most loving voice I had ever heard. I couldn't believe this was the man I had spent the last seven years of my life running from! I had been running from the wrong Jesus.

"I want you to know that I have too much for you to do, and you can't live this way," He said. Then He asked me what I wanted to do. He gave me two choices. He said, "You can *stay*, or you *die*." When He said the word *stay*, in my mind's eye, I saw a short Asian woman in a wedding dress, and a little baby girl, and I knew if I stayed I would have a family.

I told Him I didn't want to die yet.

"OK," He said. Jesus then stood next to my bed in the ER, holding His hands behind His back. "I have a present for you," He said.

"OK," I said.

> FOR THE FIRST TIME IN
> MY LIFE, I FELT DIGNITY,
> LIKE I WAS FINALLY ENOUGH
> FOR SOMEONE, AND I DIDN'T
> WANT TO SPEND ANOTHER
> SECOND WITHOUT HIM.

He brought His hand from behind His back. In it was a word in the shape of a crown—DIGNITY. "You dropped this seven years ago, and I picked it up and kept it safe for you, because I knew one day I would get to put it on you again." Then, with a knowing smile, He said, "Even with all you have done, even if you had chosen death tonight, I still would have taken you home, because even still an ember in your confused heart knows I am the Son of God."

Then He left. I reached after Jesus, trying to hang on to Him. I pleaded silently, "Don't go! Please don't leave me!" For the first time in my life, I felt dignity, like I was finally enough for someone, and I didn't want to spend another second without Him.

That night in the ER, Jesus spoke to me and gave me a choice to start over, a chance to follow Him and fulfill my destiny. I rededicated and restarted my life on that emergency room table. Jesus reached down and touched me; He saved my life with His grace.

Picking Up Where I Left Off

When I "restarted" my life, I did not have to start over from scratch—which is great news for a prodigal. Grace is so incredible that it doesn't take you back to the beginning; it takes you to the place you would have been if you had been faithful the entire time. That is how grace works in relation to destiny. Of course, I still had some very practical "starting over" things to do related to learned behaviors. Nevertheless, God still made up for lost time. He met me where I was, restored me, and then redeemed my past, with all its failures and mistakes. And I got to pick up right where I had left off with Him.

In Matthew 20 Jesus tells the story of the owner of an estate who hired workers at different times of the day to do the same job in the field. At the end of the day, the workers all got paid the same wage, though some had hardly worked. When some of the workers complained, the estate owner answered:

> Friend, I haven't been unfair! Didn't you agree to work all day for the usual wage? Take your money and go. I wanted to pay this last worker the same as you. Is it against the law for me to do what I want with my money? Should you be jealous because I am kind to others?
> —Matthew 20:13–15, nlt

The ones who got upset were the ones who had been working longer. They remind me of the older brother in the prodigal son story in Luke 15. He was upset that his young, rebellious brother was being treated as well as he was. As far as the older brother was concerned, his younger brother had already squandered everything he had, so he deserved nothing more. Even though he had come back home, the older brother thought he should be treated according to his sin and rebellion.

In both stories we see God doesn't make the last workers or the prodigal son do anything to earn their "fair" share. They aren't treated in light of their actions but in light of His goodness. Because of God's goodness, the last workers were treated as if they had been working the entire time, and the prodigal son was treated with the same love and acceptance as his older brother, as if he had never left home.

How He Loves

God chooses to dispense grace in an offensive way because of His pure, unadulterated love for His creation. He's not trying to offend; He just can't help but continue to give people chances to repent. In fact, the Bible tells us God even gave Jezebel time to repent (Rev. 2:21).

In Song of Songs 4:9 Jesus the Bridegroom says to His beloved, "You have ravished my heart, my sister, my bride; you have ravished my heart with one glance of your eyes" (MEV). In other words, God is madly in love with His creation! He is madly in love with you and me! This sort of love knows no bounds. It's the crazy kind of love that withholds nothing and gives up everything. It's the kind of love that would drive a man to continue loving and welcoming his adulterous wife home, even taking in her illegitimate kids as his own.

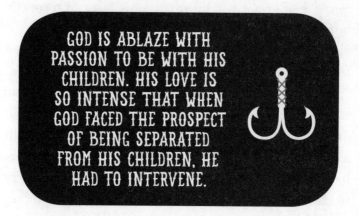

GOD IS ABLAZE WITH PASSION TO BE WITH HIS CHILDREN. HIS LOVE IS SO INTENSE THAT WHEN GOD FACED THE PROSPECT OF BEING SEPARATED FROM HIS CHILDREN, HE HAD TO INTERVENE.

In Revelation 4:3 God is described as resembling a sardius stone (MEV)—a deep, fiery red stone representing the deep, fiery passion of God for humanity. God is ablaze with passion to be with His children, even as He sits on His throne in heaven. His love is so intense that when God faced the prospect of being separated from His children, He had to intervene.

When some of the angels sinned, God didn't intervene; He simply kicked them out of heaven. But when people created in God's image sinned, God paid the ultimate sacrifice and died on a cross to redeem them. He could not bear to be eternally separated from His children. He had to do something, anything. As the Trinity—God the Father, Jesus the Son, and the Holy

Spirit—communed in heaven, Jesus volunteered: "Me. I'll go. I'll become man. I will die the most horrific death. I will be accused, and I will take all their shame and sins upon My shoulders. I will pay the ultimate sacrifice. Because of love, I will do whatever it takes to reconcile humanity to God."

The love of God is intense, and His grace often seems unfair, because He desires that none will perish (2 Pet. 3:9). God is jealous for our love and affection, and He is jealous to see us fulfill our God-given destinies. He knows the only way we can fulfill our destinies is through a deep and healthy relationship with Him. When things like sin, sickness, and disease come into our lives and try to strip us of our destinies, it enrages God. When other lovers seduce us, God's jealousy is ignited.

God's love for His children and His anger toward sin and its destruction of His children compels Him to extend grace to the most undeserving. It's as if the more unworthy we are, the more grace God gives us to enable us to repent and change, because He alone knows our true potential and the fullness of our destiny. He knit it into our DNA when He formed us in our mothers' wombs.

God doesn't care that His grace offends people. He only cares that we have all the grace we need to change so that He can lead us into the fulfillment of our destinies.

Chapter 7

PRAY FOR DAYLIGHT

SOMETIMES ALL WE NEED IS A GLIMMER OF HOPE. Hope is a hammer that smashes the bonds of disappointment—whether it's disappointment in oneself or disappointment in a loved one.

While I was struggling with hopelessness, my parents were also struggling with hopelessness. They had plenty of good days, full of faith and hope for my coming home. But they also had plenty of bad days, filled with anger and frustration. They had seasons of endlessly interceding for me, and at other times they were too tired and heartbroken to even find the words to pray. They describe it as an ebb and flow, in which they would have to reach a breaking point to reach the next level of empathy. God needed to hit them with another wave of empathy for me. At other times, they just had to rest and allow the Holy Spirit to minister to them.

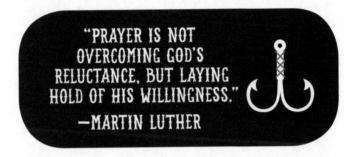

> "PRAYER IS NOT OVERCOMING GOD'S RELUCTANCE, BUT LAYING HOLD OF HIS WILLINGNESS."
> —MARTIN LUTHER

Despite their internal struggles, my parents never gave up on me, and they continued to express love to me. My father later told me he had resolved to never give up until I was dead. My parents had anchored themselves in the promise they received from God that I would be a prophet to the nations. As time went on, they put demands on that promise.

Martin Luther said, "Prayer is not overcoming God's reluctance, but laying hold of His willingness."[1] When praying for a prodigal, we have to remember that God loves that person more than we ever could. We may be desperate to see that person changed and transformed, but God is even more desperate to do the changing and transforming!

PERFECT (ACCELERATED) TIMING

All the prayers prayed for me were cashed in on one night. It wasn't because I was a prophet and could still hear God or because my father was an associate pastor. God broke in because people were praying for me. It's as simple as that. When it seemed like there was no hope left for me, when my parents had finally witnessed the extent of my depravity, God stepped in "just at the break of dawn" (Ps. 46:5, NKJV).

We may be tempted to think God doesn't hear or answer our prayers, but in Revelation 5:8 it says that before God's throne are "golden bowls full of incense, which are the prayers of saints" (MEV). And Paul reminds us:

> But, beloved, do not be ignorant of this one thing, that with the Lord one day is as a thousand years, and a thousand years as one day. The Lord is not slow concerning His promise, as some count slowness. But He is patient with us, because He does not want any to perish, but all to come to repentance.
>
> —2 PETER 3:8–9, MEV

We should never think God's delays are God's denials. We have to trust His sovereignty and believe He is willing to do what He says He will do. So many factors are at work behind the scenes, most of which we are completely unaware of, and we have to trust God to be in control.

It is a scary place to be—watching a loved one run from God—and our only option is to pray and trust God to break in. Sometimes we begin to give up on loving that person altogether because it feels easier and safer. We are often fearful of loving people who are out of control. But as long as we keep praying, we won't stop loving, because prayer joins our hearts to the one we are praying for. When you feel like giving up, press in even more!

The great news is that God's perfect timing in answering our prayers can actually be accelerated through our prayers. Bob Sorge writes, "When evil is looming we can postpone its coming with our prayers; and when good is delayed, we can accelerate its coming with our prayers."[2] He puts it another way, "Intercession accelerates God's purposes in the earth."[3] We find an example of this in Hebrews 13, when the writer urges his fellow believers to pray "that I may be restored to you the sooner" (Heb. 13:18–19, NKJV).

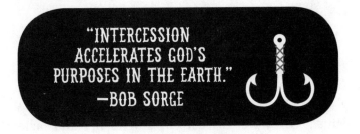

"INTERCESSION ACCELERATES GOD'S PURPOSES IN THE EARTH."
—BOB SORGE

KEEP RUNNING

I have never run a marathon, but I've heard it takes a lot of patience. You have to train for months prior, and during the race you have to pace yourself properly in order to make it to the finish line. To me, 13.1 miles doesn't exactly sound like a walk in the park. It's not like a sprint, where you just make a mad dash from Point A to Point B.

Loving a prodigal is a marathon, not a sprint. You need strength for the journey, not just a spurt of energy for the hour. Sure, it's more like a roller coaster marathon, and at times it can even resemble an obstacle course. But pace yourself, slow and steady. Jesus promised, "Keep on asking, and you will receive what you ask for" (Luke 11:9, NLT).

This is true even once your prodigal has returned home. For me, it wasn't smooth sailing immediately; it took a while for all my issues and addictions to be worked out. It was a process for me, as is often the case for those struggling with sin and returning home. It's crucial during this time to exert patience rather than tolerance. Patience means waiting with long-suffering and expectation for change. Tolerance expects no change. People almost always live up to the expectations we place on them, so if we expect change, we will see it. If we don't, we won't.

OCEANS OF PRAYERS

At all costs, we must continue to love our prodigals with the kind of love that puts darkness to shame. And we must continue to pray, whether in words or tears.

The psalmist wrote, "You keep track of all my sorrows. You have collected all my tears in your bottle. You have recorded each one in your book" (Ps. 56:8, NLT). Another name for these bottled-up tears is *liquid prayer*. Sometimes our words cannot express the aching of our hearts, so we just weep before the throne of God. We might be able to muster up a few words here and there, but the substance of this prayer is tears. I believe these prayers are some of the most sincere, because we are completely broken and vulnerable to God in this state. It is a complete surrender of all that has been weighing so heavily on our hearts—all the hopelessness, disappointment, anger, frustration, and bitterness that goes along with loving a prodigal.

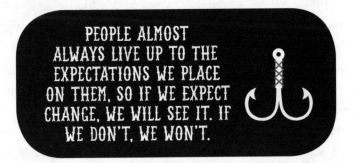

PEOPLE ALMOST ALWAYS LIVE UP TO THE EXPECTATIONS WE PLACE ON THEM, SO IF WE EXPECT CHANGE, WE WILL SEE IT. IF WE DON'T, WE WON'T.

A mighty promise accompanies these liquid prayers. "Those who sow in tears shall reap in joy" (Ps. 126:5, MEV). The word *shall* makes this a definitive promise—something we can hang our hat on. So keep praying, and keep holding fast to the promises God has given you about your prodigal. Don't give up. Dawn is on the horizon.

CRITICAL NETWORK

In addition to loved ones, it is vital for a prodigal to have a support network of leaders and other Christians. As Christians, we must be a safe place for people to make mistakes. We must love with the same kind of love Jesus had for the vilest of sinners, and we must arm ourselves full of compassion. Compassion is the armor love puts on to go out and end people's suffering.

Christians must love with a godly love rooted in truth. We must never sacrifice truth for love, but we also must never sacrifice love for truth. They must go hand-in-hand. Love without truth is not godly love but tolerance that gives excuses for sin, resulting in compromise. Godly love will never produce poor character.

Prodigals need to be reminded that God loves them and is not disappointed in them. Of course, He's upset that they're hurting themselves, because He loves them and values them. But He is not a dictator. He is a Father and a lover. He is not chasing prodigals away but running after them, pursuing them. He doesn't want to leave them the way they are; He wants to lead them back into righteousness and the fulfillment of their destinies. That's what we should want for them too.

SPEAKING DESTINY

One of the ways we can partner with God's heart in this is to continually speak out destiny over young men and women in our midst. Because "death and life are in the power of the tongue" (Prov. 18:21, MEV), we must speak as much life into young people as we can—while they're still healthy! Sure, we can wait to prophesy to dry bones, but why would we wait when we can prophesy to living bodies? Who knows whether our words will be the strength they need to avoid becoming prodigals.

One of the most influential speakers of destiny in my own life was Reggie Dabbs, the guest speaker at the church camp in Devils Lake during my sixth grade year. Reggie played such a significant role in my spiritual awakening by speaking destiny and purpose into me that I was completely starstruck with him, a black man whom I followed around like a white shadow. Reggie was so kind to me! He didn't once say or even give the impression that I was a chubby white kid who was driving him crazy. No, instead he let me carry his Bible and spoke life into me. Reggie told me I would be a great man of God someday.

Years later, when I was running from God, I remembered that experience with Reggie. From time to time, I would hear those words Reggie had spoken over me echoing in my head. I didn't believe them anymore, and I felt like a failure because I was under so much shame and condemnation. But I believe now that when Reggie spoke those words into me, he helped place me on the offensive for everything the enemy would try to do to me later. I believe his kindness toward me and his words of destiny were seeds into my life that eventually took root when I came back home.

It is easy to forget the impact and power of our words and actions, but they tend to linger, whether for good or bad. Let's partner with God in speaking good.

The Great Lost and Found Department

This was what Jesus did while on Earth. Witnessing the struggles of His creation broke His heart and so moved Him with compassion for people that He seemed to spend nearly every waking hour speaking life, healing the sick, and casting out demons. He would minister from sunrise to sundown, using the early morning hours as His retreat with God. When He did sometimes try to retreat from the crowds by crossing lakes and rivers, He was always met on the other side by another crowd. And He couldn't turn them away.

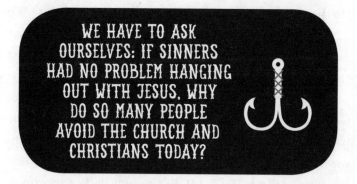

WE HAVE TO ASK OURSELVES: IF SINNERS HAD NO PROBLEM HANGING OUT WITH JESUS, WHY DO SO MANY PEOPLE AVOID THE CHURCH AND CHRISTIANS TODAY?

When Jesus wasn't healing the sick or raising the dead, He was either preaching to the multitudes or hanging out with sinners. He was not intimidated by the labels placed on the outcast men and women who interacted with Him. In fact, He preferred them over the religious scribes. That is how the body of Christ should be too—so driven by the Father's heart of compassion that we give of ourselves unreservedly, like workers in a great lost and found department. To do that, we need to be a safe place where people can fail.

We have to ask ourselves: if sinners had no problem hanging out with Jesus, why do so many people avoid the church and Christians today? Jesus never tried to make sinners feel good, and He never led them to believe He was OK with their sin. In fact, He often confronted them about their sin. But He bathed His words in love and compassion, and they never got offended. The only people who got offended were the religious. Jesus was able to truly love sinners, despite their sins, without compromising the truth. Somewhere along the line, the church has forgotten how to do this. We have lost sight of the burning heart of God for the lost, and we no longer really know how to love people past their sins.

We urgently need to reconnect with the heart of God for the lost and the prodigals. We need His same passion, relentlessness, and fervency so that, like Him, we will leave the ninety-nine sheep in search of the one lost sheep (Matt. 18:12–13). In the first half of this book, I told the story of my journey from lost to found. In the second half of this book, I want to look at what it takes to be people who will go after the prodigals and love them into restoration. This is our Father's heart—that the sons and daughters who are at home in His heart would help Him bring the lost and prodigal children home too.

Part 2

LOVE LIKE A HURRICANE

Chapter 8

HURRICANE LOVE

WHEN SONGWRITER JOHN MARK MCMILLAN compared God's pursuing love to a hurricane, he reminded us of the fierce and transformative nature of that love. God's love like a hurricane can truly take the most wretched sinners and make us into righteous sons and daughters of God. Like a cyclone, it picks us up and shakes us around and sets us down in a new and better place, stripping us of the old lies that held us back and reminding us of who He made us to be. That's what God's love hurricane did for me, and it's what He can do for anyone who has wandered from his home.

John Newton, who wrote the famous hymn "Amazing Grace," knew a thing or two about the hurricane love and amazing grace of God. During the 1700s, John Newton was a slave trader who was radically saved while captain of a ship transporting slaves. After his conversion, Newton abandoned the slave trade and became a preacher and evangelist, and later became an abolitionist and even the spiritual director to William Wilberforce, the man credited with convincing the British Parliament to outlaw the slave trade.

He understood the power of God's grace to take a person from absolute wretchedness into incredible destiny. John Newton is a model of just how much God loves to restore. Like the unheroic heroes of faith, the filthy fishermen, and me, Newton saw God take the places where he'd failed most and turn them into something purposeful and powerful.

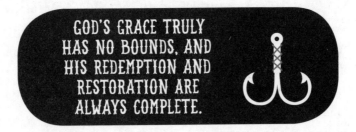

GOD'S GRACE TRULY HAS NO BOUNDS, AND HIS REDEMPTION AND RESTORATION ARE ALWAYS COMPLETE.

Each of these stories of the amazing grace of God points us to the unfathomable reality of God's goodness available to us all. It's not just for biblical characters or people called to play a significant role in history. It's for ordinary people like me and my friends and you. Just when we're tempted to think someone might be impossible to redeem and restore, God steps in and says, "I got this." The following stories from the lives of a few friends of mine are proof. The grace of God truly has no bounds, and His redemption and restoration are always complete. Meet my friends Lisa, Hank, Susan, and Amanda.[1]

LISA

Lisa's husband was a pastor, and for four years she lived out her dream of being a professional singer, traveling the world with a Grammy award–winning gospel artist. Then Lisa decided to take a break in order to be a pastor's wife and have kids. As with many women, though, Lisa gained weight after giving birth to her kids. Soon she became so obsessed with losing her pregnancy weight that she turned to a drug called crystal meth.

Sure enough, four months after her initial hit, Lisa was sixty pounds lighter. But along with her weight she had lost her marriage, her children, her home, and her car. Her parental rights had been revoked, and she had nothing, yet she refused to get help.

In her lowest moments, Lisa cried out to God, meth pipe in hand, "Oh God! I can't do this anymore. Save me from myself! I can't do this on my own!" Not long afterward, Lisa discovered she had become pregnant with a doper's baby. She decided that day that she would not use crystal meth with a baby growing inside of her. Surrounded by a strong support group, with intercessors praying on her behalf, Lisa became sober.

In order to stay sober after her pregnancy, Lisa decided to move to a small town where she knew no one. She managed to get a job that barely supported her and as a result left her no room for drugs. Since Lisa knew no one, her evenings were extremely lonely and usually ended with her crying herself to sleep, thinking of the life she once had and wishing she could take it all back.

Then one day she heard a pastor say from the pulpit, "If you always do what you've always done, you'll always be where you've always been." Lisa decided that night to start reading her Bible again. She started out slowly, reading one verse a night and saying a quick bedtime prayer. As the weeks passed, she began to develop a hunger for more, and she began to feel comfort in her moments of loneliness.

One night she asked God to make her content with being single, to help her make Him and her children her sole focus. She added, "If You have someone special for me, make him more in love with You than with me so that he can see me through Your eyes."

IF YOU ALWAYS DO
WHAT YOU'VE ALWAYS
DONE, YOU'LL ALWAYS
BE WHERE YOU'VE
ALWAYS BEEN.

Two days later Lisa received a phone call from Sam, a safety manager from out of town whom she had never met or spoken to before. What began as a business phone call ended with them exchanging cell phone numbers and e-mail addresses. Over the next three days, Lisa and Sam spent between eight and ten hours a day on the phone together. Their conversations were filled with talks of God's goodness and His anticipated restoration in both of their lives. Sam had also been divorced and had run from God for some time. When they prayed for several days about their relationship, both received the same word: restoration! Six weeks after their initial conversation, they were married.

Lisa relocated to live with her new husband, and after she spent six months unsuccessfully trying to find a job, Sam advised her to do something she had always wanted to do but couldn't. Lisa enrolled in cosmetology school. As one of the older students, Lisa soon found herself acting as a mentor to many of the younger students, and she began seizing every opportunity she could to speak about God.

Five years have passed since Lisa took her last hit. Today Lisa is walking in security and fulfillment. She enjoys a thriving marriage and is able to spend quality time with each of her children. She also leads the young adults in worship each week at her church.

Lisa says, "It's not about what I've lost; it's about what I have gained through the redemptive and restoring character of Jesus Christ."

HANK

My friend Hank married his beautiful high school sweetheart. She was a cheerleader, and he was a punk rocker. They lived in a big house and had three kids together. Hank and his wife had been youth pastors at one time, but they were exposed to the dark side of ministry. The church had mistreated them. Now Hank had a cushy IT job at a prominent company, and everything seemed to be going really well for Hank and his family. In fact, they had just sold their house, with plans of purchasing an even larger one. He seemed to be living the dream.

Then one afternoon, I received a call from Hank unlike any other I'd ever received from him. His voice shook so badly I could hardly understand him. I could tell he had been crying for a while. Without going into details on the phone, Hank asked if there was any way I could meet with him. I agreed.

Twenty minutes later, I found myself sitting across from Hank at a restaurant. When I had walked in, Hank had his head bowed low and was noticeably trembling. I soon found out why.

Hank had gotten fired from his cushy IT job when they discovered pornography on his work laptop during a routine sweep. He confessed to me that he had been addicted to pornography for over twenty years, but he had never told anyone. The story got worse. Hank's laptop had been confiscated and turned over to authorities, and they had uncovered what appeared to be images of underage girls. Hank's shaking became more violent as he continued his story.

Hank had no choice but to confess his addiction and the reason for his termination to his wife. They ended up needing to move into a small, three-bedroom apartment, since they could no longer afford the new house and had already sold their current one. Thankfully, the police concluded there was no child pornography on Hank's laptop. But his marriage was in shambles, and he was jobless, with two preteens and a toddler. Hank repented to his wife and God, and he entered counseling for his pornography addiction. He recognized the ordeal as God's mercy and grace to expose his addiction—for the sake of his family and his future.

Six months later Hank was able to land another job at another well-respected company—this time making even more than what he was making previously. As a result, he and his family were able to get an even bigger house than both the one they had sold and the one they were planning on buying. Today, Hank and his wife have been married sixteen years, and he says his marriage has never been healthier.

SUSAN

Susan's parents were godly, Spirit-filled Christians, and she attended private Christian schools until she reached ninth grade, when her parents allowed her to

attend a public high school. By the end of her sopho-
more year in high school, Susan had met her first boy-
friend: Jonathan.

Susan and Jonathan were in love. They obsessed
over one another, and after a few months of dating they
started having sex. Susan knew better, but she rational-
ized her sexual relationship because she had every inten-
tion of marrying Jonathan. But by the next year, she and
Jonathan had broken up because her family moved to
another town. Still, Susan and Jonathan remained sexually active, despite his decision to date another girl.
Because Susan was still in love with him, she justified
her actions.

Susan graduated high school at seventeen and
moved in with her sister to attend a nearby college. She
lived closer to Jonathan now, and even though he was
still dating that other girl, the two began having sex
on a more regular basis. They had devised a system to
avoid pregnancy, but Susan decided it was time to get on
birth control when she turned eighteen. Per her doctor's
orders, she had to wait until after her next cycle to start
the pills. But it never came.

Susan purchased and took three different pregnancy
tests, which all came back positive. Later, her mother
also made her take another three pregnancy tests, which
also all came back positive. At eighteen, as a freshman
in college, Susan was pregnant. Her father told her to
give the baby up for adoption; her mother, believing a

fetus was not a baby until after six months, told her to have an abortion.

When Susan told Jonathan, he also told her to get an abortion. Susan was devastated. She didn't want to have a baby so young, but she also didn't want to abort her child. Her anguish was so great she wound up having a mental breakdown on the front steps of Jonathan's apartment.

Susan's mother convinced her to go to Planned Parenthood the next day. Susan knew abortion was wrong, and she kept looking for something to help her make the right decision. The night before her visit to Planned Parenthood, Susan prayed, "Father, I have screwed this up so badly! Please help me do what You want me to do. Don't let me make any more huge mistakes! Lead me in what to do that is right!"

The next day at Planned Parenthood, as she lay on the bed for an ultrasound, Susan prayed another prayer, begging God to help her make the right decision.

Suddenly, the technician conducting the ultrasound stopped and wiped the gel off Susan's stomach. She called Susan's mom in as Susan sat up. The technician said she could not find a baby and asked if they were sure Susan was pregnant. The technician explained that they normally can see the fetus by the fourth week of pregnancy, but by this time, Susan was already close to eight weeks along. The technician said there was no sign of a fetus, and she asked Susan to come back in a few weeks to try and detect the fetus then.

Susan was relieved! God had answered her prayer, and there was no way she was going back to Planned Parenthood! She was going to have this baby.

Today, Susan's son is twenty years old. He is a gift from God, and she thanks God every day that He kept His hand on her and her son's life, hiding her son from the shadow of death. Despite her youthful promiscuity, her mother's ignorance, and Satan's deceptions, Susan and her mother loved and trusted in the Lord. And He was faithful to step in and save them, not only from themselves but also from the enemy.

AMANDA

Amanda was raised in a blended Christian home. Her parents had both been married with two children prior to marrying each other. Amanda was the only mutual child between her parents. She was also the youngest in the family, with all her half siblings being eight to eleven years older than her.

At a very young age, Amanda was molested by one of her half brothers on several occasions. After her mother found out and confronted her half brother, it never happened again. But Amanda never dealt with the incidents, and she began to struggle with sexual issues and promiscuity throughout her adolescent years.

At eleven years old, Amanda first opened the door to the homosexual stronghold that later took root in her life. By the time she was thirteen, Amanda had become sexually active. She gave birth to her son when she was eighteen, and she was married to her husband at nineteen.

Amanda and her husband regularly invited pornography and sexual promiscuity into their marriage and even opened the door to bringing others into their bedroom. From the first time they invited another woman into their bedroom, Amanda was never able to be intimate with her husband again without fantasizing about being with a woman.

NONE OF US ARE ABOVE HIS GRACE; WE ALL BADLY NEED IT. ONCE WE HAVE BEEN REDEEMED, OUR JOB IS TO TELL THAT STORY OF REDEMPTION!

Fifteen years into their marriage, Amanda had a final affair that brought her sexual addiction issues into the light, and she and her husband committed to doing whatever they needed to make their marriage work. Amanda began to deal with the addiction she had toward men, attention, and open sexual acts, and she and her husband stopped watching pornography. Instead, they plugged back into church and got their lives back on track with God. But rather than deal with her feelings of attraction for other women, Amanda suppressed them, figuring there was nothing wrong so long as she didn't act on them.

Several years later, while doing a corporate fast with her church, Amanda felt directed to fast from any sex with her husband. On the second day of her fast, the Holy Spirit began to deal with the bonds of homosexuality that had formed in Amanda, which she thought she had been born with. By the end of the fast, the homosexual strongholds were broken from Amanda's life, and today she not only has no desires, tendencies, or fantasies about women, but her relationship with her husband is "normal" and much more loving than ever before.

The testimonies of Lisa, Hank, Susan, and Amanda are among millions of redemptive stories in the lives of everyday people. Nearly every Christian I know has an amazing story of God's grace and redemption. None of us are above His grace; we all badly need it. Once we have been redeemed, our job is to tell that story of redemption! We get to give God the glory for the awesome and wonderful things He has done for us.

If your redemption has not yet come, hold on, for it is drawing near. Cry out to God—your Savior, redeemer, and restorer. Cry until He breaks in. And when He does, shout it from the rooftops for the world to hear!

> I waited patiently for the LORD to help me, and
> he turned to me and heard my cry. He lifted

me out of the pit of despair, out of the mud and the mire. He set my feet on solid ground and steadied me as I walked along. He has given me a new song to sing, a hymn of praise to our God. Many will see what he has done and be amazed. They will put their trust in the LORD.

—PSALM 40:1–3, NLT

Chapter 9

IMPLAUSIBLE
RESTORATION

NOT LONG AGO I HAD A PHONE CONVERSATION
with a friend of mine who is a pastor in another
state. He told me about the issues they were having with
a worship leader at his church. Because of what the worship leader had done, the church leadership had decided
to remove him from his position so they would not be
associated with him. As I listened to my friend, I wrestled internally with what I was hearing. Even though his

decision is a common one in churches today, Jesus never acted this way with His disciples, and He doesn't act that way with us either. Jesus was desperately committed to helping people find healing and restoration, even unto death. But I kept these thoughts to myself and allowed my friend to talk.

A few weeks went by, and I decided to call my friend to see how the situation was progressing. He told me they had made it official and removed the worship leader. Suddenly I had an idea. I told him we were having the same issue at the church I was helping lead. I told him we had a worship leader who was very famous and known all over the world. We had just hired him, but we had a problem.

"What's the issue?" my friend asked me.

I told him this worship leader was in a very dark place and had had an affair with a married woman.

"Oh man," my friend said. "Get him out of there before your reputation suffers!"

"It gets worse," I said. "This worship leader actually fell in love with this married woman, and she got pregnant."

This sent my friend through the roof, and he was adamant about publicly expelling this worship leader.

"It gets much worse," I told my friend.

"How could it get any worse?" he asked.

"Well, this worship leader tried to cover his own tracks, and we just found out he had the husband of the woman killed."

"That worship leader will never be in ministry ever again!" my friend declared. Then he asked me for the name of this worship leader so he could make people he knew aware.

I told him, "His name is King David."

My pastor friend was beside himself. He simply could not believe what had just happened. He was silent for a moment, and then said, "I understand. Thank you."

King David was an implausible case for restoration. He broke the biggest rules in the book, yet God went against all our ideas of what should happen and who should be in ministry, and He restored David. He did not remove him from leadership of His nation but confronted him about his sin and restored him to a place of righteousness. And after David's death, he became known as a man after God's own heart.

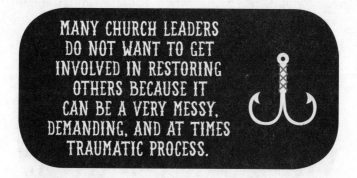

MANY CHURCH LEADERS DO NOT WANT TO GET INVOLVED IN RESTORING OTHERS BECAUSE IT CAN BE A VERY MESSY, DEMANDING, AND AT TIMES TRAUMATIC PROCESS.

What's even more amazing is that God still loves this kind of crazy restoration of His fallen sons and daughters today. However, many of us find it absolutely terrifying. We don't know what to do when people make such big messes, and we feel afraid. That's why we are so quick to respond like my pastor friend and distance ourselves from the offending person as quickly as possible. Many church leaders do not want to get involved in restoring others because it can be a very messy, demanding, and at times traumatic process.

Sexual sin is one of the most common reasons people need restoration. It is the number one catalyst the enemy uses to knock people out of their positions of authority. Not surprisingly, restoring those who have fallen because of sexual issues can be particularly difficult and messy simply due to the complex nature of sexual brokenness. It is most pastors' "worst nightmare," but it's not God's. He is not afraid of the messes His children make. Many men in the Bible and throughout history have fallen for this very reason—including the great King David. And when those who fall repent, God's heart has always been to restore.

GOD IS NOT AFRAID OF THE MESSES HIS CHILDREN MAKE. WHEN THOSE WHO FALL REPENT, GOD'S HEART HAS ALWAYS BEEN TO RESTORE.

Unfortunately I have met with many pastors who would rather turn a blind eye to the issues in their churches than confront what is opposing the kingdom's expansion in their community. This is a tragic misunderstanding. Restoration is not just about an individual being restored; it is also about the kingdom being established in a community or church. It is the business of the Cross, and we all need it. We all are in desperate need of a savior. We need to be reminded of the importance of restoration. We must be brave enough to face the mess and love the mess-maker, and we must clearly communicate the need for restoration when Christians fall into sin. When we gloss over this truth, we make it easy for people to hide from their need to repent and be restored. Because of their wounds and deception, they believe they can continue in a lifestyle of sin.

This is not what God wants for His children. He wants all of us to be free from sin and to live in our destinies, but we cannot do it alone. We need one another. When one of us falls, the rest of us need to pick that one back up and remind that person of who he is called to be. This is the model God the Father and Jesus gave us. God is a God of restoration, and with Him the situations in which restoration seems implausible certainly are not impossible.

The dictionary defines restoration as "a return of something to a former, original, normal, or unimpaired condition" or "something that is restored, as by renovating."[1] Synonyms include alteration, cure, healing, rebuilding, reclamation, recovery, reestablishment, reformation, rehabilitation, rejuvenation, remaking, remodeling, renewal, renovation, return, and revival.[2] From this definition we can see that restoration is a really amazing thing. Those who have fallen from their royal position in the kingdom can be put back into that position and experience greater glory through that reestablishment.

The synonyms for restoration bring a deeper level of understanding that otherwise would be lost. Revival is one of the synonyms for restoration; not only are people put back into their position, but they are repositioned *in revival.* Being reestablished to their former glory in the very spirit of revival means a restoration to life, consciousness, vigor, strength, and so forth. Not only do they get back into their position, but they also get strength and consciousness, which means sobriety and character.

Here we see the fruit of restoration done right—strength and character. If someone is restored to leadership yet is racked with insecurities about that position, the reconciliation was not done correctly—either by the one restoring or the one being restored. If the individual being restored has an unhealthy amount of self-persecution and shame, that person's heart didn't connect with the true process and the true reason for the restoration.

Conviction, grief, guilt, and repentance are only appropriate before we ask for forgiveness, not after we have been forgiven and restored. When we are forgiven for a sin, it is no longer necessary to keep repenting for that same sin. We must then walk in confidence in the strength of the Lord and His ability to truly forgive.

Restoration can only happen in the context of true forgiveness. When a fallen leader repents, God will forgive him. Then he needs to forgive himself, and those who are trying to restore him also need to forgive him. Without these three sources of forgiveness, real restoration is not possible.

THE PERFECT PROCESS

Churches often bring our ministry in to assist with cleanup after leaders experience moral failures. The principal question asked in these situations is, "Is there one perfect way to restore someone?" The answer is *yes!* The perfect model for restoration is to treat each individual who is being restored as a unique person with unique issues. We get into trouble when we try to make everyone fit into a mold of restoration. We want a simple, one-size-fits-all plan to make the issue go away as quickly as possible, but it just doesn't work that way.

Restoration is a customized process, because every person is unique. What succeeds with one person may not succeed with others. Our goal is not to rush people through a restoration machine but to lovingly heal their hearts. It's like the difference between being repaired in a factory and being nursed by a doctor.

I know the process of restoration because when I was a young man I walked through restoration. Now, looking back, I see the huge flaws—as well as the good—in the process I experienced. Even though it was completely messy and a lot of big mistakes were made in the process of my restoration, God worked it for my good. Along the way, I learned what not to do when restoring someone else. It has proven a priceless tool to me, and now one aspect of our ministry is restoration for individuals, relationships, and churches.

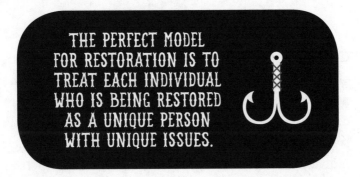

THE PERFECT MODEL FOR RESTORATION IS TO TREAT EACH INDIVIDUAL WHO IS BEING RESTORED AS A UNIQUE PERSON WITH UNIQUE ISSUES.

This process of restoration, though it is customizable to each individual, must follow some important standards that provide a framework to assure a healthy and complete restoration.

1. The person needing restoration must choose to submit to the process.

This is the starting place. If people have control over their own process of restoration, it is proof they are not really in the restoration process. When people have fallen and submit to restoration, they are saying, "I trust You, Jesus, with what I have done, and I trust those whom You have given charge over me." That means when people are being restored, they don't get to enter into contractual negotiations to the tune of, "You can restore me, but here are my concessions." The whole point of entering into restoration and submitting to others is based on people's admission of their own deception in a certain area, which has caused them to stumble into an unhealthy lifestyle or has brought injustice to their families. Implicit in this admission is the need to submit to others' directions until that deception is overcome and the individuals are once again able to see clearly.

However, the flip side is that people who need restoration should not submit to a system that is unhealthy, cultish, or violating to their free will. God will never violate our free will, and neither should the process of restoration. Those who need restoration should seek it in a healthy and safe environment, and then they should fully submit to those who have agreed to restore them in that environment.

When people submit to restoration, it means they are doing so of their own free will. In other words, they need to freely choose it, not be forced into it. Unfortunately many people enter restoration because of fear; this, I believe, is the major reason restorations often don't go as planned. When individuals submit to restoration with deception in their hearts, they enter into the process not with free will but with fear or wrong ideas about what will take place. Such fear and wrong ideas can spring from fear of separation, rejection, or isolation.

Instead of fear, the ideal entry point is trust. When people accept their need for restoration by trusting others with what they've done, they are entering the process with free will. Without trust, true submission to the process is impossible. It will always be motivated by fear or an unhealthy agenda. As leaders, if we want people to trust us with their restoration process, we must be trustworthy people. It is a big responsibility to be trusted so fully concerning what is good and healthy for another individual.

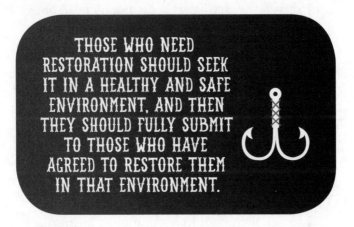

THOSE WHO NEED RESTORATION SHOULD SEEK IT IN A HEALTHY AND SAFE ENVIRONMENT, AND THEN THEY SHOULD FULLY SUBMIT TO THOSE WHO HAVE AGREED TO RESTORE THEM IN THAT ENVIRONMENT.

2. Several trustworthy individuals must be involved.

For healthy restoration to happen, it must involve more than two people. The one primarily responsible for restoring the fallen person must be accountable to others who are wise and mature in such areas. It doesn't work to have an immature believer navigate the complex process of restoration. It is always better to have a few people in on the process. That doesn't mean everyone needs to know the depths of what has landed an individual in restoration, but it does mean those who are brought into the process must keep an eye on the situation to assure no abuse, on any level, is happening. This is in the best interest of everyone involved.

3. Rely on the Word and the Spirit.

The process of restoration must be conducted by God through the wisdom of the Word and the leading of the Holy Spirit. It cannot be left to people alone. Otherwise, these people will most likely break the fallen person's spirit. As humans, we just don't know exactly what each person needs to find healing. Only God knows each one of us well enough to know that. And only He can orchestrate the restoration process in a truly healing and freeing manner. Without His guidance, we will rely on formulas or opinions, and we will end up creating even deeper wounds in the person we're trying to restore.

As I mentioned previously, every person will have a unique process. When we listen to the Holy Spirit and rely on God's Word, we will be able to discern the best process for each individual. Some people need very strict guidelines because of the measure of darkness they have come into agreement with. Others need lower boundaries because they committed a lower level of offense. Some people will not come out of their wounds and deception without being shaken loose. For others the deception is not as deeply rooted, and therefore the time they need to reach wholeness is much shorter and the process is much simpler. Truly, we need the wisdom of God when walking saints through this sensitive process.

4. Establish healthy boundaries.

Part of the restoration process is the establishment of boundaries to help people heal and find freedom from deception. As mentioned in the last section, some people will need really rigid and high boundaries, and others will need lower boundaries. While some churches come down very hard on those who have fallen, others seem afraid to bring any actual correction. Both extremes are harmful. When someone in the church community is continually harming others, high boundaries are an absolute necessity.

Restoration is not about a legalistic list of dos and don'ts, but if there are no boundaries, there is no process of restoration. Restoration is not about punishment but about helping someone overcome a poor behavior based on personal deception. The way to help people overcome their poor behaviors is through asserting godly boundaries. The cure for poor behaviors related to deception is godly boundaries.

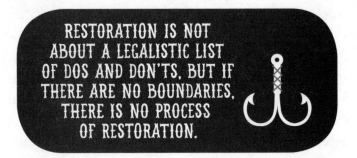

RESTORATION IS NOT ABOUT A LEGALISTIC LIST OF DOS AND DON'TS, BUT IF THERE ARE NO BOUNDARIES, THERE IS NO PROCESS OF RESTORATION.

Sometimes when people are going through the process of restoration, they may feel like boundaries are legalism. We must remember to discuss this aspect of restoration with those who are being restored. Our goal is never to control sin in others. That is not the purpose of creating boundaries. This is why we need to ask the Holy Spirit for help concerning where the boundaries are needed. Only He knows what each person needs in order to truly overcome the area of struggle instead of simply controlling his or her behavior through legalism.

5. Say no to shame.

As we set healthy boundaries designed to help the person succeed and find freedom, we must be very careful to never put shame on an individual. Before someone repents, God can use guilt to lead that person to repentance. Guilt is a public emotion that causes us to confess our sins to God and people, but shame is a private emotion that causes us to become more isolated and broken. We should never shame others; and when someone has repented, we should not put guilt on that person either. We see this concept in Galatians 6:

> Brothers, if anyone is caught in any transgression, you who are spiritual should restore him in a spirit of gentleness. Keep watch on yourself, lest you too be tempted. Bear one another's burdens, and so fulfill the law of Christ. For if anyone thinks he is something, when he is nothing, he deceives himself.
>
> —GALATIANS 6:1–3

Many have used this passage as a weapon to put shame on those going through restoration. I have been in leadership meetings and heard well-meaning pastors make statements like, "Be careful restoring that brother, because if you're not careful, you could fall into the same sin he is caught up in." However, when we read these verses with a proper understanding of the nature and character of God, we will see that what the Lord is really saying doesn't have anything to do with falling into the same sin. Instead, it is a caution to restore someone with a spirit of gentleness in order to avoid falling into judgment against the individual being restored. The danger here is not a copycat sin but the sin of judgment, which too often causes church leaders to shame those who have fallen instead of calling them into their destiny in God.

6. It is OK if it gets a little messy.

Finally, we must accept the fact that restoration was never meant to be a simple and clean process. Consider the crucifixion of Jesus Christ—the ultimate act of restoration. There was nothing simple or clean about the process of crucifixion. The bottom line is, restoration can be messy and painful. People sometimes get hurt in the restoration process because as imperfect humans we are addressing sometimes significant wounds and deceptions in people's lives. But all the mess is worth the joy of seeing people freed from deception and empowered to live in their destinies as healthy individuals. It is a fearful and wonderful opportunity to assist fallen brothers and sisters in being restored to the Lord and to the community. To be the sort of people who can guide others through restoration, we need to be personally healthy and, like Jesus, be driven by the Father's heart for all His children.

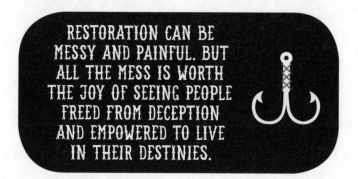

RESTORATION CAN BE MESSY AND PAINFUL. BUT ALL THE MESS IS WORTH THE JOY OF SEEING PEOPLE FREED FROM DECEPTION AND EMPOWERED TO LIVE IN THEIR DESTINIES.

Chapter 10

THE FATHER'S HEART

WE WILL NEVER HAVE A PROPER ATTITUDE toward prodigals and sinners if we do not understand the Father's heart. In Jesus's parable in Luke 15, it was the father who waited for and welcomed home his prodigal son, and it is the Father who sent His beloved Son Jesus to bring His lost children home to His heart. Thus Jesus came to Earth to reveal God as the Father and to offer us restored relationship with Him by dying for our sins on the cross.

Even from the beginning, God had a Father's heart

and wanted a family to share His love; that was why He created humanity. But the intimacy He desired was thwarted (for a time) by Adam and Eve's decision to rebel against their Father. Now that Jesus had come to provide a way for the prodigal children to come back home, He needed to show them what their Father was really like. Just like me, they had believed lies about who God is and what He wanted from them. They needed to see Him for who He really is.

IF WE UNDERSTAND JESUS'S TEACHING, MISSION, AND PERSONALITY, WE WILL KNOW THE FATHER.

The idea of God as a Father was completely revolutionary. The Jews saw God as the transcendent creator of Genesis 1; they kept their distance and trembled before Him. But Jesus revealed God as a Father with great affection, commitment, and desire for close relationship. Jesus emphasized the affectionate, deeply involved, relational dimension of God's personality as a Father, and He invited all people to draw near to this kind, tenderhearted Father God with confidence.

The Bible tells us Jesus is the "exact representation" of Father God (Heb. 1:3, NIV). In other words, if we understand Jesus's teaching, mission, and personality, we will know the Father. To read the Gospels, to see what Jesus said and did, and to interpret His words accurately, is to know the Genesis 1 God as our Father. Jesus showed us exactly what He is like.

The fact is, Jesus's personality, ministry, and teachings were profoundly attractive to the disciples and the people of His day. They enjoyed being in His presence, and Jesus told them the Father was just like Him. If they knew the Father, they would be drawn to Him and enjoy being with Him, just as children enjoy being with their earthly fathers. Though they would tremble before God's great power as Creator, they would also feel confident and safe in God's presence because of His great affection for them as a Father.

DADDY GOD

When we turn back to Father God, He gives us the Holy Spirit, who lives inside us. This Spirit reaches out to God the Father through us as the Spirit of adoption, enabling us to cry out, "Abba, Father" (Rom. 8:15). *Abba* is an intimate term of endearment like *Papa* or *Daddy*. It is respectful yet affectionate and intimate. As the Spirit of adoption, the Holy Spirit reveals to us the glory of our position as adopted sons and daughters of God. He convinces us of the truths and benefits related to being adopted children of God. Adoption implies a legal position of privilege in which the child becomes an heir of the family name, resources, and estate. Through our new position as adopted children, we have access to the Father's heart in a unique way. The Spirit convinces us we can encounter God as our Abba. This "Abba revelation" is so important because it empowers us to endure difficulty and to reject Satan's accusations against us. It is what enables the prodigal to come back home.

Amazingly the measure of the Father's love for Jesus is the measure of His love for us (John 17:23). This is the ultimate revelation of our worth, giving all believers the right to view themselves as "God's favorite." When I was a prodigal, I believed God could not love me because I had failed Him, but the exact opposite was true. The Father feels about each one of us in the same way He feels about Jesus. He will not increase in His love for Jesus, and He will never love anyone more than He loves Jesus. Therefore, since He loves us the same way, He will never increase or decrease in the measure of His love for us. We all need a deeper and continual revelation of this truth. The Holy Spirit is eager to guide us into this truth about the Father's love; all we need to do is ask (John 16:13). Our lives are broken and unsettled, without a stabilizing anchor, until we know the embrace of the Father as our Abba. We need the assurance that God delights in us even in our weakness. When we really know this, we will be confident and whole in His love, and we will learn to give out that same love to the lost and hurting.

UNEARNED LOVE

When we operate in legalism or performance, we expect God to love us based on our gifts or abilities or maturity. We think what we do for Him will convince Him to love us, but that is a lie. Father God's heart is full of love for us, no matter what we are doing or who we are. He loves the most spiritual person and the least spiritual person the same, because a good father loves all his kids, regardless of what they do. He loves them because of their identity as His children, and that identity cannot be removed by poor decisions or weakness.

When His lost kids return home, God immediately rejoices over them, even while they are incredibly immature. He smiles over every one of us as we begin the growth process, long before we attain maturity, because He does not confuse spiritual immaturity with rebellion. Newly repentant yet immature prodigals still have many areas in their lives in need of transformation. But God is not focused on their weaknesses, withholding His love until they get it together. Instead, He feels gladness and enjoyment in His prodigals on the day they repent.

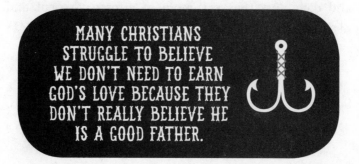

MANY CHRISTIANS STRUGGLE TO BELIEVE WE DON'T NEED TO EARN GOD'S LOVE BECAUSE THEY DON'T REALLY BELIEVE HE IS A GOOD FATHER.

We see this in Jesus's parable of the prodigal son.
The prodigal's father made his acceptance of his repentant son known by giving his prodigal son the best robes
and the family ring on the day he returned. This is so
important for us to understand as we relate to prodigals.
Just like our Father, we need to fully embrace and love
them at the moment of repentance, not wait until they
reach maturity to accept them.

See, the parable of the prodigal son is not primarily
about a son who lost his inheritance but about a father
who lost his son and how the father gets his son back.
When we sincerely repent, we can have a new beginning
with God as first-class members of His family. The act
of repentance is like pushing delete. We are no longer
seen according to our past failures but according to the
nature of Christ. Thus, we are enabled to relate to God
on the terms laid forth in His Word—on the basis of
who God is, who He says we are to Him, and how we
are to relate to Him. The Spirit of Jesus the Son lives in
us, and through Christ we build relationship with our
Father in heaven. The same confident love, privilege, and
assurance Jesus enjoyed are offered freely to us as sons
and daughters the very moment after we repent and
receive salvation.

A GOOD FATHER

So many Christians struggle to believe we don't need to
earn God's love because they don't really believe He is a

good Father. The truth is, the vast and magnificent God of the universe has always been in love with us. When He decided to create humanity, God put His hands into the clay of the earth and formed a person. He was and is a hands-on Father. He is not a distant Father who just stops by every once in a while to make sure we are OK. No, He is deeply involved in the process of our lives.

Unfortunately, because of our own brokenness and the poor examples set by our natural fathers, it's not always easy for us to relate to God as our Father. It is not always easy for us to believe He is good and kind. Nevertheless He is who He says He is—a good Father full of mercy, compassion, truth, power, affection, and desire for a whole and healthy relationship with us. He longs for us to live out our destinies as bold and confident sons and daughters.

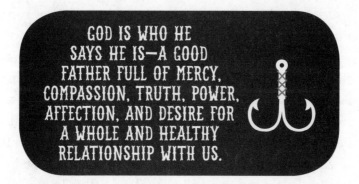

GOD IS WHO HE SAYS HE IS—A GOOD FATHER FULL OF MERCY, COMPASSION, TRUTH, POWER, AFFECTION, AND DESIRE FOR A WHOLE AND HEALTHY RELATIONSHIP WITH US.

We cannot exaggerate the importance of knowing God as a good Father. In fact, the discovery of God's emotions toward us is one of the most significant revelations of our spiritual lives. Our answer to the question,

"How does my Father feel when He looks at me?" will change everything, because what we think He feels determines how we approach Him, especially in our weakness.

THE GLAD-HEARTED GOD

One significant emotion in our Father's heart is gladness. We will struggle to comprehend His affection for us until we have a foundational understanding of His gladness. The Father's capacity for gladness is both infinite and eternal, and He also designed our human spirits with great capacity for gladness. As we become students of God's gladness, we grow in revelation of His tender affection for us. A revelation of God's gladness will change us in three significant ways.

First, when we stumble in sin, we will run to Him with confidence and sincere repentance instead of running from Him in condemnation and shame. Second, we will love the prodigals in a way that genuinely reflects the glad-hearted Father. Third, when we realize our Father possesses the fullness of joy in His presence (Ps. 16:11; Rev. 4), we will become confident in our joy. It will become our strength (Neh. 8:10), enabling us to be joyful in all circumstances. When stressful situations arise in my life, I close my eyes and picture my Father in heaven, and I'm settled and comforted when I see gladness in His place (1 Chron. 16:27).

THE FATHER WHO THINKS OF YOU

Another powerful reality of the Father's heart is His promise, "I think of you." He governs all of creation, yet He thinks of us. When I'm going, when I'm coming, when I'm sleeping, when I'm traveling, when I'm at home, when I'm working—He thinks of me. Jeremiah 29:11 says, "For I know the thoughts that I think toward you, says the LORD, thoughts of peace and not of evil, to give you a future and a hope" (NKJV). It's almost too good to be true.

David had firsthand knowledge of the thoughts of God about him. In Psalm 139:17–18, he wrote: "How precious to me are your thoughts, O God! How vast is the sum of them! If I would count them, they are more than the sand." Similarly Psalm 40:5 says, "Your thoughts toward us cannot be recounted to You in order; if I would declare and speak of them, they are more than can be numbered" (NKJV). David knew God's thoughts toward him were good, and because of this, he was named by God as "a man after His own heart" (1 Sam. 13:14).

THE THOUGHTS OF THE FATHER OVER US ARE INSPIRED BY HIS DELIGHT IN US. HE TAKES GREAT DELIGHT IN EACH ONE OF US.

Scripture is full of God's thoughts toward us. In Psalm 16:3, David wrote on God's behalf, "As for the saints in the land, they are the excellent ones, in whom is all my delight." Likewise, Job declared of the righteous man, "He shall pray to God, and He will delight in him, he shall see His face with joy" (Job 33:26, NKJV). Isaiah the prophet declared to God's people, "you shall be called My Delight Is in Her, and your land Married; for the LORD delights in you" (Isa. 62:4). Moses also declared these promises over God's people: "The LORD your God will make you abundantly prosperous in all the work of your hand.... For the LORD will again take delight in prospering you" (Deut. 30:9). The prophet Jeremiah likewise spoke God's heart for His people: "I will rejoice in doing them good...with all my heart and all my soul" (Jer. 32:41). And Zephaniah cried out:

> The LORD your God is in your midst, a mighty one who will save; he will rejoice over you with gladness; he will quiet you by his love; he will exult over you with loud singing.
>
> —ZEPHANIAH 3:17

Reading these verses, we cannot doubt God's delight in every one of His sons and daughters. Instead, we can apply our names to each of these verses and declare them back to God. When we hear the words and speak them with our mouths, the process of belief speeds up in our hearts, impacting our feelings and thoughts about God. Truly, the thoughts of the Father over us are inspired by

His delight in us. He takes great delight, pleasure, enjoyment, and joy in each one of us. We don't have to work for the kingdom to earn His delight. Love is simply who God is. He loves us, and this love awakens love for Him in us and inspires us to serve Him because of love, not out of a need for approval (1 John 4:19, John 3:16).

THE TRUSTWORTHY FATHER

He is such a good Father, a trustworthy Father who is not out to trick us (Luke 11:11–13) but to love us to life. I spent seven valuable years of my life running from God, lost in drug addiction and hopelessness. During those years, I could hear the Father speaking over me and calling me back to Him, but an orphan spirit kept my ears and heart deaf to His love. I needed to see Him as my Father, not the director of an orphanage, before I could return home to Him. Orphans who have not reconciled their wounds will kick against anyone who is trying to be a father to them, and that is exactly what I did. But when the Father pursues that orphan relentlessly, eventually that love-motivated pursuit will overcome that orphan spirit!

> THE FATHER *NEVER* GIVES UP ON US. HE WANTS TO CRAWL INTO OUR FAILURES WITH US SO HE CAN PULL US OUT OF OUR MESS.

When I was twenty-five and lying on an emergency room table, dying of a drug-induced heart attack, Jesus—the revelation of the Father—came to me. The first thought I had when I saw Him was, "What did I just spend seven years running from?" I had spent seven years running from the wrong Jesus. I had spent seven years rejecting the wrong Father. He is not a bad Father. He is a loving Father who *never* gives up on us. We have a Father who wants to crawl into our failures with us so He can pull us out of our mess. Because of His great love, He is not afraid to get His hands dirty! A true understanding of His love for us, as a good Father, will enable us to find out who we really are in Him.

FINDING OURSELVES IN HIM

If we don't feel like treasured children, it's a sign we don't really comprehend God's heart. It's a sign we are not living in His presence, which is full of joy. Only in His presence will we find our true source of identity. Only there will we find peace in who we are in Him.

One time my wife, Grace, and I went to Bethel Church in Redding, California, for a leadership conference. We were both so excited to be at a place where we felt in one accord with the culture and community. I found myself thinking things like, "This is where God will encounter me and deal with all my issues." But there is a fundamental problem with this kind of thinking. It produces shame-based worship. Our first reaction to the presence of God should not be shame but hope. I used to come into the place of worship and lift my hands to the Lord and instantly start thinking of all the ways I had failed all week. I would just stand there saying sorry for all the broken ways I'd walked in.

Then the Holy Spirit spoke to me about this, "Luke, please stop doing this! Stop letting Satan rob God."

"What do You mean?" I asked Him.

He answered, "When your heart is postured in worship and all you do is think of your failure, you are worshipping your failure and giving life to the darkness." The Holy Spirit wanted me to stop worshipping failure, because it was producing more failure in my life. We worship what we fear. What a profound revelation.

SEEING HIM FOR WHO HE IS CAUSES US TO BECOME LIKE HIM.

At Bethel the worship was amazing! My wife has this uncanny ability to step right into God's presence in worship. I, however, take some time to clear my head and enter in. So Grace's hands went up and her tears started flowing, but I was feeling absolutely nothing. I thought, "Something's wrong with me because I don't feel anything."

Right then the Father said to me, "Let's go for a walk, baby boy."

I was angry and thought to myself, "Hey! This is where You are right now. What do You mean, 'Let's go for a walk'?" After arguing with the Father for a bit, I left my seat and began walking out while still grumbling about leaving the service.

As I walked into the lobby, the Father said, "Listen to Me now. You were afraid to come here because you thought this was the place I deal with all your little issues. Luke, I know all your issues, and not a single one of them intimidates Me. I knew you would have the struggles and weaknesses you have from before anything ever was. [See Ephesians 1.] What troubles Me as a Father is not your issues; it's the fact that you are not confident in who I have called you to be!"

This blew my mind and brought the tears right out of my eyes. His main concern was seeing me operate out of who I am in Him, not how I fail. I am not saying repentance and obedience aren't important. That's not my point here. The point is, He cares more about my heart than He does about my weakness. When my heart is connected to His in love and trust, my weaknesses become much more manageable because they come under the influence of His love.

We see this reality in the "beholding and becoming" principle from 2 Corinthians 3:18: "And we all, with unveiled face, beholding the glory of the Lord, are being transformed into the same image from one degree of glory to another." In other words, whatever we behold (meditate on) in God's heart toward us becomes awakened in our hearts back toward God (transformation). Seeing Him for who He is causes us to become like Him.

To behold God's heart means studying about it, speaking about it, and praying it until we understand it and therefore encounter truth and are changed and transformed on the inside. As we change our minds (understanding) about God, He changes our emotions and unlocks our hearts to love more. In this way, we are empowered to walk in greater righteousness as we grow in our understanding of the love of God.

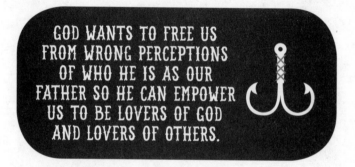

GOD WANTS TO FREE US FROM WRONG PERCEPTIONS OF WHO HE IS AS OUR FATHER SO HE CAN EMPOWER US TO BE LOVERS OF GOD AND LOVERS OF OTHERS.

Conversely wrong understanding about God damages our hearts and causes disability in our walk. God wants to free us from wrong perceptions of who He is as our Father so He can empower us to be lovers of God and lovers of others. The way He does this is by revealing Himself as a lover to us. As we encounter His love, we are changed into His likeness, and we become those who can in turn partner with Him in loving other lost sons and daughters back to the Father's heart.

Chapter 11

THE MASTERPIECE

WHEN WE FIND OUR IDENTITY IN FATHER GOD'S heart, we discover something amazing. He prizes us as His *masterpiece*. Right after Paul writes about salvation as a gift of grace, he explains the why behind that gift—because we are God's masterpiece. "For we are God's masterpiece. He has created us anew in Christ Jesus, so we can do the good things he planned for us long ago" (Eph. 2:10, NLT). This realization changes everything. It changes the way we see ourselves, and it changes the way we see others. It enables us to be the sort of people who can welcome the prodigals home and help restore them to wholeness.

The almost unbelievable truth is that God looks at us, with all of our shortcomings and imperfections, and declares us His masterpiece. When God surveyed all His creation—colors, stars, galaxies, mountains, oceans, creatures, and so much more—He decided we humans are the pinnacle of His creation, the work He's most proud of. It's hard to believe when we look at the magnificence of creation, but it's true. Humanity alone is the chosen masterpiece, the favored creation in whom God chooses to dwell and to whom He entrusts His presence. We are, after all, made in His image. As David wrote:

> You made all the delicate, inner parts of my body and knit me together in my mother's womb. Thank you for making me so wonderfully complex! Your workmanship is marvelous—how well I know it.
>
> —PSALM 139:13–14, NLT

I imagine God literally sitting there, knitting us together, one by one. First, He picks out our hair color, eye color, height, body type. Then, He forms our personalities and passions around a specific destiny He has chosen for each of us. He adds in likes and dislikes, talents and hobbies. He numbers our days and accounts for any and all of life's mishaps and our own screwups. He turns us over and over, inspecting every fiber in our

DNA, and adds some final touches. When He's completely satisfied, He steps back and smiles at another masterpiece. I can see angels crowding Him and the four living creatures surrounding Him, all *oohing* and *ahhing* over His latest creation.

It is no wonder that when God was looking for something to give His Son as an inheritance, as any good father would, He chose His masterpiece. To a Son who had everything, God gave you and me (Ps. 2:8). We are not just God's masterpiece but Jesus's inheritance! We see this in Jesus's prayer just moments before His arrest: "Father, I desire that *they also, whom You have given Me,* be with Me where I am, that they may see My glory which You have given Me" (John 17:24, MEV, emphasis added). Paul also mentioned this: "That you may know what is the hope of His calling, what are the riches of the glory of *His inheritance in the saints*" (Eph. 1:18, NKJV, emphasis added).

Understanding who we are to God—the masterpiece—is so important. In fact, I am convinced that losing sight of this is what causes some of His children to wander from home. They forget their identity as His masterpiece, and they don't know what He says about them. When they hear the enemy's taunting accusations, they think it's God's voice, and they believe it—just like I did. It's time we as the church confront these lies with the truth of who God says we are.

THE FORGETFUL GOD

A few years ago I ministered at a powerful prophetic conference. During the altar call, I noticed an older gentleman with a wry look. When I approached him, he challenged me. "If you can tell me exactly what I did thirty years ago that made me go to prison, I'll believe God has truly forgiven me," he said.

I paused and asked the Holy Spirit to tell me what he had done.

Silence.

"Well?" I asked the Holy Spirit.

"Um...I don't remember," He finally whispered.

I was shocked! "What do You mean, You don't remember?" I asked the Holy Spirit. It was such a cop-out answer, I thought. I mean, it was such a simple thing this man asked for, and in exchange, he would believe.

"I don't know what to tell you," the Holy Spirit said. "I don't remember."

I sighed. I was a little upset at the Holy Spirit and a little embarrassed to face this man. I didn't know what to tell him, and he was starting to get impatient.

"I'm really sorry," I said, shrugging as I turned toward him. "I asked the Holy Spirit, and He said He doesn't remember."

Suddenly the man started sobbing uncontrollably. I later found out this man's entire family had shunned him when he was arrested for this crime, a crime that required him to register on a national database every time he moved anywhere. In fact, his wife had ended her life as a result of this atrocious crime. While society would hold his past crime against him for the rest of his life, God chose to remember it no more.

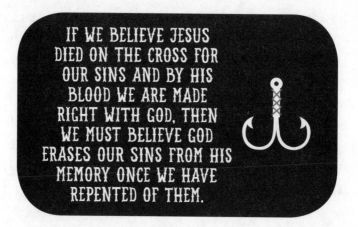

> IF WE BELIEVE JESUS DIED ON THE CROSS FOR OUR SINS AND BY HIS BLOOD WE ARE MADE RIGHT WITH GOD, THEN WE MUST BELIEVE GOD ERASES OUR SINS FROM HIS MEMORY ONCE WE HAVE REPENTED OF THEM.

That's exactly what God does when we repent of a sin: He blots it out of His memory (Isa. 43:25; Heb. 8:12). David, a man well acquainted with sin, wrote, "As far as the east is from the west, so far has He removed our transgressions from us" (Ps. 103:12, MEV). This is the fact we need to embrace, the message the prodigals need to hear. Either we believe the entire Bible, or we believe none of it. If we believe Jesus died on the cross for our sins and by His blood we are made right with God, then we must believe God erases our sins from His memory once we have repented of them. The omniscient, all-knowing God who is outside of time chooses to forget the sins we have repented of.

He does this because of His great love for us as His

masterpiece. He does it because He's our Father and because He made us to be beautiful and amazing.

DARK BUT LOVELY

We often define ourselves and the people around us by our present circumstances, but when God looks at us, He sees with an eternal perspective. He sees us twenty or fifty years down the line. He sees us according to our destiny. We may be darkened by sin in our present, but God looks at us and calls us lovely, because He knows who we really are—His masterpiece. He is not turning a blind eye on our sins; after all, He is a holy God. But He sees beyond our present struggles and deep down into our hearts, and He rejoices in the *yes* of our hearts before we walk it out in obedience. Truly He is the "God, who gives life to the dead and calls those things which do not exist as though they did" (Rom. 4:17, NKJV).

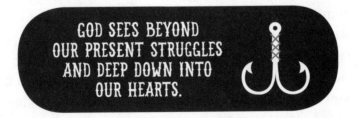

GOD SEES BEYOND OUR PRESENT STRUGGLES AND DEEP DOWN INTO OUR HEARTS.

When viewing ourselves and others, it is important for us to know that God does not have human eyes but dove eyes. In the Song of Songs, a metaphorical book about Jesus the Bridegroom and His bride, the church, the bride describes her beloved's eyes as "doves beside springs of water; they are set like jewels" (Song of Sol. 5:12, NLT). Doves have no peripheral vision, and they have one mate for life. With no peripheral vision and a fierce loyalty to their mate, doves do not get distracted by the things going on around them. When a dove looks at its mate, it sees only its mate—nothing else. This is what God is like toward us.

When Jesus the Bridegroom looks at you and me, He doesn't get distracted or swayed by the things going on around us. His gaze is intently directed at our hearts, not our sin. Even if we are struggling with sin, He recognizes us as sincere lovers of God who are struggling with sin, not as sinners struggling to love God. The difference is significant, because if we know who we are, we can start pursuing our destinies. Even if we struggle with sin, we must realize God still enjoys us, and we must be able to say, like the bride in Song of Songs, "I am dark but beautiful" (Song of Sol. 1:5, NLT).

When we really understand this to be true of ourselves, we can begin to see others in the same way. We can look at them with the Father's dove eyes and ask Him to help us see the fallen the way He sees them. This is so important because it enables us to recognize every person as a masterpiece, no matter what that person has done, and to see every person according to destiny. This is exactly the vision we need to help restore the fallen to righteousness.

RECOVERING DESTINY

Lately God has charged me to call the church into a place of hope, identity, and breakthrough. Many in the body of Christ are dealing with great grief and letting the hurts, failures, and mistakes of their past determine where they go in the future. But God wants us to align ourselves with our true identities as His children. God desires to give us good gifts, to bless us, and to give us a future. God wants to heal us of our painful history and help us find our identity in Jesus. And He wants us to help others do this too.

After returning to the Lord, I still struggled with some major issues. They were real "deal breakers" concerning my walk with the Lord. As I struggled with these issues, my focus slipped from God to myself, and I started to be consumed by my past. I was reacting to pain and difficulty in the way wounded people often do. Here's how it happens. When we are thinking from a wounded perspective (as I was), it is easy to take our focus off Jesus and who He created us to be. Without even realizing it, we become more inwardly focused and give much of our energy to pacifying hidden wounds. When we do this, we lose ourselves in the issues we struggle with instead of finding freedom and healing. It's like drinking salt water. The more one drinks, the thirstier one gets. The more we pacify our wounds, the farther we get from who we are in Christ. We drink, but we die of thirst.

When we focus on our disappointments and failures, we begin to lose ourselves, and we start to agree with deception. I define deception as simply believing a lie about oneself or about God. Both forms of deception produce the same fruit—delusion, a control-based way of achievement. We look at our wounds, and we are not sure if God is good or if God is aware of our pain. Overwhelmed with disappointment, we begin to try to control our path to destiny. But delusion and control will never help us reach our destiny. The deceptions we believe about ourselves and God will pervert our dreams and hopes. *Destiny* is God's dream for our lives, but *delusion* is based on our pain and disappointments. Our unresolved wounds are fuel for delusion, steering us off the path of destiny.

The key to unlocking our destinies is leaning on our identity in Christ. One day as I was talking with the Holy Spirit, He said to me, "Low self-esteem is the number one killer of pastors." In my study I found that low self-esteem dictates our path to delusion. By contrast, understanding our true identity empowers us to walk down the path to our true destiny. When we don't believe we are enough for God or pleasing to God, we begin to doubt our worth. Our vision becomes skewed, and we start feeling like we need to make ourselves valuable instead of believing we are already valuable to the Lord.

> OUR UNRESOLVED
> WOUNDS ARE FUEL FOR
> DELUSION, STEERING US OFF
> THE PATH OF DESTINY.

First, our identity must be established in our relationship with God. This happens as we encounter His thoughts and affections toward us. When we are confident in our relationship with our Father and His love for us, we will not be waiting for the other shoe to drop. Instead, empowered by His love, we will overcome the negative aspects of our history and start to walk in confidence and with purpose. If we agree with heaven and literally start to declare biblical truths about who we are before God, our hearts will soften and become accessible for healing.

Going Back for the Future

One time, in a vision, I saw a large group of people lined up in front of me. The Holy Spirit showed me how He literally went into each person's past. First, the Holy Spirit went in through the eyes of a woman in front of me. He took me to this woman's bedroom when she was a child. She was lying on her side on her bed, crying, and as I watched, the Holy Spirit cupped His hands around her feet and breathed into His hands. Slowly, the little girl began to light up with a warm glow, as if light was coming from inside her and glowing through her skin. I then returned to stand in front of this grown woman. Tears were rolling down her face as she said, "I forgive you, Dad." The Holy Spirit had literally gone back in time to when she was an abused little girl, and He had healed that place in her heart.

Next, I saw an older man standing in line. Again I went on a journey with the Holy Spirit and saw a much younger version of this man sitting on his sofa, sobbing. His wife was explaining to him that she didn't love him anymore and was leaving him for another man. The man was left alone, crying on his couch, as she said good-bye. Then I watched as the Holy Spirit rushed to him, put His hands around this young man's heart, and breathed. Just as had happened with the young girl, this young man was filled with a warm glow. Again, I returned to stand before the older man, now with tears rolling down his face. As he looked straight forward, he said, "I forgive you, sweetheart."

This was happening with everyone in line. They were all allowing the Holy Spirit to go deep into their pain, hurt, and disappointment to heal them. God then said to me, "I am literally going back in time for the sake of your future." He gave me a vision of everyone in the line standing with luggage in their hands. At the front of the line was an airplane with the word *Acceleration* written on its side. A voice from heaven said, "If you're boarding the promises of God, you have to check your baggage." The luggage was too big and heavy to take on board this airplane of acceleration. Each person needed to hand his or her luggage over to Jesus before boarding. As people chose to give Him their luggage, He took it, and they were free to board.

The point is clear: we need to let go of the baggage in our lives in order to move forward with God. He is dedicated to taking us into our future as healed and restored individuals. We need to choose to be brave and allow the Holy Spirit to go into our past so we can be made whole and released into our future, so we can live out our identity as masterpieces of God! When we release past wounds and failures, choose to forgive, and decide to trust Jesus with our past, present, and future, God will restore us to our destiny.

THE POWER OF THE BLOOD

The problem for many of us is that it's very hard to accept God's unconditional, unchanging love when we live in a constant state of shame and condemnation about the past. But as Bob Sorge poignantly writes, "Why should you be surprised at the extravagant, unconditional affections of the Father for you? You have the blood of Jesus upon you!"[1]

I remember looking in the mirror one day, and my reflection talked back to me. It told me to kill myself, that there was no hope left. I believed it, because I didn't think God could love me in the state I was in. I had idolized my sin and had become consumed with shame and hopelessness. Condemnation leads to idolatry. It causes us to focus so much on our sins that we devalue the blood of Christ. When we condemn ourselves, in essence we are saying our sins and failures are greater than God, and we end up worshipping our sins rather than the God who died on the cross to erase our sins.

WE NEED TO LET GO OF THE BAGGAGE IN OUR LIVES IN ORDER TO MOVE FORWARD WITH GOD.

The Bible tells us we become like what we worship (2 Cor. 3:18).[2] When we continually behold our sins rather than God's glory, sin becomes our identity, we sink deeper into shame and condemnation, and we give up on our destinies. However, if we really believe Jesus paid the ultimate sacrifice by dying on the cross for our sins, we have to believe nothing is greater or stronger than His blood. Jesus died on the cross for every past, present, and future sin. That means every sin we have repented of belongs under the mighty power of Jesus's blood. Repented sin is "under the blood" and can never legally be used for accusation, shame, or condemnation—by humans or any other being.

> WHEN WE CONTINUALLY
> BEHOLD OUR SINS RATHER
> THAN GOD'S GLORY, SIN
> BECOMES OUR IDENTITY,
> WE SINK DEEPER INTO
> SHAME AND CONDEMNATION,
> AND WE GIVE UP ON
> OUR DESTINIES.

This is our identity in Christ! We are the masterpiece of God, and the beloved inheritance of His Son. For we were not "redeemed with corruptible things, like silver or gold...but with the precious blood of Christ" (1 Pet. 1:18–19, NKJV).

Chapter 12

BRAVE-HEARTED LOVE

AN UNDERSTANDING OF OUR IDENTITY AS THE Father's masterpiece and His heart of love for all His children is the necessary foundation for true, brave-hearted love. This is the Jesus kind of love that bravely lays down its life for others. This kind of love is sadly lacking in the church, but it is exactly what we need to bring the prodigals home.

I wish I could say I learned what real, brave-hearted love looks like while growing up in the church and reading my Bible. But I can't. Instead, my first lessons in love came in the form of an early boyhood crush on a girl down the street, a friendship with a sick boy named Adam, and a chance to live with a disabled young man named Carl. My personal response to each of these friends taught me something important about brave-hearted love.

SOUP DOWN THE STREET

Let's start with the girl down the street—a little Vietnamese grade school classmate of mine. She and her family lived down the street from me, and I loved playing at her house and eating her mom's traditional Vietnamese food. There was only one problem standing between me and this little girl—the House.

Along the several blocks between my house and hers stood a little house (a shack, really) inhabited by two alcoholic sisters and their dog. These sisters were old and mean, like their mean, old dog. This dog, which my friends and I were convinced had supernatural powers, barked and bellowed, shaking the plywood that covered the windows like a terrifying mystery. None of us had ever seen the dog, but our young minds were convinced this demon hound had consumed many children from our neighborhood.

To see my Vietnamese classmate and eat the bounty of her family's kitchen, I had to pass by "the House" where "the drunk ladies" (as we called them) and their demon dog lived. I remember standing just down the street from the House, butterflies twirling in my stomach, thinking about what would happen if the drunk ladies or their dog ever came out while I was walking by. Despite the prospect of terror (in my mind), my desire to see the girl I was sweet on would embolden me, and I would work up the courage to race down the sidewalk as fast as I could till I had passed the House. The comfort of my friend's smile and a warm bowl of Vietnamese soup did it for me every time.

In this way I learned that love means being brave. When we face hard circumstances, the reward for bravery is the power to overcome again and again. The brave-hearted lovers are the ones who will overcome hurdles to love and refuse to allow fear or inconvenience to distance them from the ones they love. The bravery we need is a combination of mental resolve and powerful emotion. Without emotion, we will never make the hard choices to persevere and overcome in pursuit of love.

> BRAVE-HEARTED LOVERS REFUSE TO ALLOW FEAR OR INCONVENIENCE TO DISTANCE THEM FROM THE ONES THEY LOVE.

Our human emotions are lively, raw, and beautiful. They are not to be feared but valued. So many Christians are terrified of emotion and spend much of their lives repressing how they feel because they believe God is repulsed by human emotion. But this is a terrible misunderstanding. God is the one who gave us our personalities and emotions when He made us in His image. He is an emotional God who was driven by passion to take crazy risks in pursuit of the children He loves. When we are reconciled through Christ, our emotions are baptized under the blood of Jesus Christ too. This means our emotions are no longer a hindrance but rather an asset for our good and fulfillment. They embolden us to live passionately and brave-heartedly in love for God and others.

We will live in greater boldness, power, and longevity in the kingdom if we embrace who Christ is in us—including how He manifests in our emotions. Some people like to quote Jeremiah 17:9, "The heart is deceitful above all things...," as proof that we cannot trust our emotions because they are wicked. The truth is, this verse refers to the unredeemed heart. But we have the heart and mind of Christ; therefore, it does not refer to us. That doesn't mean our emotions are always right. We must continually lay our bodies, minds, and spirits before the Lord and allow the Holy Spirit to transform us. But it does mean that allowing ourselves to feel and admitting when we are hurt or disappointed is healthy and important, not wicked. When we repress our emotions, we miss out on experiencing the heart of God, and we will be very handicapped in our ability to love like He loves.

God wants us to be present and awake in this life, not to live as emotionally numb sleepwalkers who are never emotionally present and therefore cannot really make an impact in the lives of those we love. I have spoken with generals of the faith who are at the twilight of their lives, and many have the same deep regret—that they were not truly present in their lives and circumstances. To be present in this life means to be fully alive, hearts beating wild and free and emotions fully baptized by the Holy Spirit.

RISKING LOVE

Of course, the reason so many people are terrified of wholehearted emotion is because it hurts like crazy when you lose someone you love. This is why when people become very sick, we tend to pull back. We are afraid of the pain of really loving someone we might lose. But real, brave-hearted love risks loss in pursuit of the loved one. It is a selfless love that cares more about the connection than about the pain that may come. I learned about this firsthand over the summer of my sixth grade year.

I was a rambunctious, fun-loving kid growing up in a middle class neighborhood, and the summer was what my friends and I lived for. Summer was when we could spend our days in carefree fun, no homework and no worries. But that summer would be different for me. One day my parents introduced me to a young man named

Adam. When I first met Adam, I could tell something was different about him. He looked different from the other friends I had. He was very tender and kind, and he was the first friend I had ever had who was dealing with a disease. Most of my friends were relatively healthy kids, so meeting someone who was sick was not normal for me. That summer, I spent quite a few nights hanging out with Adam, and I learned a lot from him—especially about brave-hearted love.

Loving someone is always a risk. We just realize it more when that person is sick. It reminds us of the vulnerability of the relationship. Relating to people who are sick is often difficult because of our own fear, bias, prejudice, or lack of education. Often we don't understand what illness can do to people, both mentally and emotionally, and we forget the importance of empathy, compassion, patience, and positivity. The same could be said for loving prodigals. But Christ calls us to love bravely, to think outside ourselves in order to serve others in a place of great need.

Psychology tells us people tend to reject the people and situations they don't understand. This is mostly due to fear, not cruelty. People tend to lash out at what they are afraid of, including sickness. When faced with a sick person, they think something like: "If you are sick or dying, then that means that same thing can happen to me. I could become sick and die, and then what would happen to those I love?" We as human beings become fearful when confronted with the fact that our lives on this earth are but a vapor, and we will do whatever it takes to get as far away from that reality as possible. We push sick people away because we are fearful of our own mortality. But God wants us to be driven by brave-hearted love, not fear.

I could have blown Adam off and never looked back. I could have refused to go over and hang out with him because it was different and awkward for me due to my lack of understanding. But I didn't. Adam had cancer, and he did not have long to live, but I decided I wanted to be his friend.

CHRIST CALLS US TO LOVE BRAVELY, TO THINK OUTSIDE OURSELVES IN ORDER TO SERVE OTHERS IN A PLACE OF GREAT NEED.

One evening, when spending the night at my pastor's house with Adam, I finally worked up the courage to just talk to him about it all. I asked questions that would have been offensive if I hadn't been a totally naïve child. Adam let me look at his portable IV and feel his bald head. He had lost all of his hair from the chemotherapy, and his head was soft and smooth. I asked him if he was afraid he was going to die. He looked at me and said, "Yes, I am afraid." I had never had such a heartrending conversation in my young life. I cried with Adam, afraid for him and what his future looked like.

Soon after our conversation, Adam and his family returned to their home in Arizona. I didn't hear from him for a while. Then one night, at the beginning of my seventh grade year, when I came home from a dance at school, my parents asked me to sit down at the table in the kitchen. I could feel something wasn't right, and my stomach began to turn. My dad and mom said, "Honey, there is something we need to tell you...Adam died today." I remember crying so hard at the kitchen table for the loss of my friend. It was the first time I had ever experienced the loss of someone I loved.

Though I didn't understand it all at the time, I now realize how much I learned from my short friendship with Adam. I learned that love is not about reward but about something much greater. Love is an open hand, an ongoing giving motion that is always overflowing. Love does not grasp on to others possessively and protectively. It loves with a brave and open heart. It gives with no expectations, just like Jesus does.

LOSING CONTROL

Years later, in the midst of my prodigal season, I met another young man who taught me a little more about brave-hearted love. At the time, I lived with a sweet and awesome family, full of love, very human, and impressively brave. This family also provided in-home care for a young man I'll call Carl, who was severely mentally and physically disabled. Though he was fifteen years old, doctors said he only had the understanding of a seven-year-old. Once I got to know him, I discovered Carl was an amazing young man who loved to laugh and was so much fun to be around.

At first, however, I was put off by Carl; I felt nervous and queasy when around him. See, all his food had to be blended, and then someone had to feed him, which involved a lot of choking and spit up. It was not an enjoyable experience to watch. However, as my heart grew fonder of Carl, the things that initially troubled me didn't seem as important.

Then one day I had to feed Carl. This was a true test for a young man with a weak stomach and good memory. Feeding Carl was brutal. All his coughing, laughing, and spitting up had turned the room into a culinary war zone. Partway through the meal, when my disgust at feeding him had faded and I started talking to him normally, he calmed down, and the rest of the meal went down without a problem.

Over the months that followed, I grew closer to Carl. Sometimes the children of my host family and I would take Carl to the mall or the movies or just hang out with him. One day we were getting Carl ready to go to the mall. There was another worker with Carl in the driveway, and I was getting ready to go outside when I remembered I had forgotten my jacket upstairs and quickly ran to get it. When I got to the second level of the home, I stopped and paused to look out the big bay window that overlooks the cityscape. Then I looked into the yard and driveway where everyone was waiting for me. As I watched, suddenly Carl's wheelchair started rolling forward ever so slightly. Then, in a breath, Carl and his wheelchair went rocketing down the hill. Carl's wheelchair hit the curb, and he was thrown into a small quarry of jagged rocks next to a fence. It all happened so quickly, yet it seemed like I was watching in slow motion.

As I stood in the living room watching, I was completely frozen, knowing I could not do anything to stop what was happening. The family rushed Carl inside and called 911. I heard someone scream for me to come to the basement, where they had just brought Carl into the bathroom. I walked down the stairs really afraid of what I might see. As I came around the corner, I saw them beginning to wash the blood off him. His blood turned the water bright pink as he cried out in pain.

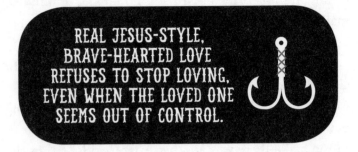

REAL JESUS-STYLE, BRAVE-HEARTED LOVE REFUSES TO STOP LOVING, EVEN WHEN THE LOVED ONE SEEMS OUT OF CONTROL.

When the ambulance workers came bursting through the door to get Carl, my eyes filled up with tears, and I thought, "God, please!" It was a simple, broken, heartfelt prayer from a prodigal for a friend he loved. They rushed Carl to the emergency room, and we drove straight to the hospital to be with him. When we got there, we waited for a long time in an off-white hallway with chairs until the doctor finally came and said we could see Carl. When we entered his room, we saw him smiling and happy to see us. Amazingly Carl didn't have a single broken bone, only a few minor stitches and scrapes. But he had taught us all a valuable lesson that day: love sometimes means having no control.

This is the essence of real Jesus-style, brave-hearted love. This kind of love is brave enough to run past danger in pursuit of the loved one. It risks loss in order to fully embrace the loved one, even if that one is in a very difficult place. And it refuses to stop loving, even when the loved one seems out of control. This is real love, brave-hearted and open-handed love. This is how Jesus loves us, and it's how we must love each other. It's the only way to love prodigals.

Chapter 13

LOVE AT THE CENTER

I SAT IN A MEETING ONCE, AT A MINISTRY I SERVED in for a number of years, where the topic of discussion was the purpose of rewards in heaven and our time and service here on Earth. An enthusiastic young man began to tell us how much he loved going out to feed the homeless or bless others. He said the reason he did this and kept it secret was because he believed every time he served it would add to his treasure in heaven.

I sat there totally shocked that this idea was being introduced in our leadership meeting. Eventually I spoke up: "If love is not our primary motivation, then serving others doesn't count as a Christian act. It takes nothing to serve because of the promise of monetary compensation, either here on Earth or in heaven. Love must be the compass that guides us to serve others."

In response, the senior leader said, "We humans are selfish by nature, and the idea of rewards is all that will truly motivate us. If we serve at all as humans, it's because we receive." In the end they labeled me an idealist because I believe love must be our primary motivation for serving others. Unfortunately these leaders are not alone in their belief that humans cannot be motivated by love to serve but only by selfishness. The truth is, once we are filled with the Holy Spirit we *can* serve from the place of love. Love serves with an open hand that does not seek selfish desires. It is the very nature of God, because God is love, and God has put His own nature inside us.

Imagine a young man meets a young woman who is everything he ever wanted in another person. He asks her out on a date, and she says, "Well, it is socially acceptable that I accept this request, so I believe I will go with you on a date." After a response like that, I think he might feel like he no longer wants to go on a date with this woman. Or imagine a husband and wife are discussing the wife's heartfelt desire to keep the house in order. In response to her request, the husband says, "Well, I am married to you, so I will clean up the house because that is what is expected of me." How would that wife feel? Would this answer satisfy her? The answer is no, of course, because though her husband is meeting her need, he is doing it out of obligation rather than love. And we all want people to do things for us and with us based on love, not expectation. Obligation is not the same thing as choosing to serve out of love. Understanding this is important in all relationships, and especially in our relationships with the lost and the prodigals.

FIRST, WE MUST LOVE GOD

But in order to do this, we first need to be motivated by love in our relationship with God. For too long the church has lived out of obligation to the Lord rather than real relationship with Him as a Father and King. So many people are sitting in church pews totally numb toward the Lord on the inside, totally unmoved by the love He has for them. We have become those who stumble around in the dark grasping after any sign of salvation and love. The truth is that Jesus is present in our lives. He is not an absentee landlord but a God who is deeply involved in our lives and hearts. We can run around confusing being busy with having real relationship, but often we are just busy and completely missing real intimacy with God.

When our heart connection with God is revived, He fills us with His love and enables us to work *from* love rather than working *for* love. We serve and love other people because we've been so filled up with our Father's love and it overflows from within us. We make the hard choices and pour out our lives for others because of love. That must be our center. By His grace, it can be.

I have discovered this in a very real way in my own life and my journey in ministry. When I first started ministering, I thought, "Man, this is amazing, and I hope I can make it big someday and speak at all the major conferences. Wow, wouldn't that be amazing?" My young heart had the wrong motive for ministry, and the Lord has spent the last decade working it out of me. In the process, I have lost my desire to be great so I can sell teachings or books. The only real way to be promoted in the kingdom of God is through God Himself. He knows when we're ready to serve in love, when we've caught the rhythm of His heartbeat.

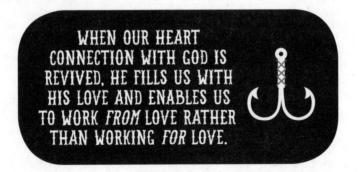

WHEN OUR HEART CONNECTION WITH GOD IS REVIVED, HE FILLS US WITH HIS LOVE AND ENABLES US TO WORK *FROM* LOVE RATHER THAN WORKING *FOR* LOVE.

One time Grace and I were invited to minister at a conference in a small town. I was very excited about the opportunity and had great expectations (delusion and pride) about this conference. The Lord had given me an awesome prophetic word for the church there and the entire city. I could hardly wait to go and deliver the word. I spent time praying and getting myself ready for this event. The day we were leaving, I could hardly sit still because I had all these ideas about the great things I would do while I was there. Don't get me wrong. I was not completely prideful. Most people would have had no idea I felt or thought this way, but in my heart, I knew it was an area of pride.

When we arrived in the town, we met the pastor and his wife at the hotel they had booked for us—which turned out to be small and dirty. I was not really excited about staying there, but I thought, "Oh well, Lord. Thank You anyway for this room." Then the pastor and his wife took us out to eat at a place some might refer to as a dive. I was actually a little nervous to eat the food (kind of like a Pharisee). Afterward, they dropped us off at the hotel for the night, and I voiced my reservations about ministering at this church.

My wife, Grace, is exactly her namesake; she is full of wisdom, prophetic insight, integrity, and grace. She told me maybe I just needed to be thankful for what the Lord was doing with us. Oh boy, was she right! I have learned so much from my wife in relation to character. The Lord has used her to help make me a better husband, minister, and all around person. After this conversation, we went to sleep, ready for the next day.

I woke up in the morning and thanked God for whatever He was doing with this event. I told Him I just wanted to be used by Him, and I gave Him permission to do a work in my heart and character related to these issues. I felt peace from the Lord about my perspective, and I felt ready to bring the word of the Lord at the event. The pastors picked us up at the hotel, and we drove to the church. As we pulled up to the church, I saw a run-down little building. I was not being critical; it was really rundown and dilapidated by most people's standards.

As we walked up the steps to the one-room building, I started to feel the Holy Spirit tug on my heart for these people and that community. I asked the Holy Spirit to help me see how He sees and to give me the strength to please God throughout the ministry I do for Him. We walked into the building, where we found about fourteen people sitting in little metal chairs and waiting for us to arrive. I had my assistant with me, and we set up our resource table, which was hilarious considering the number of people there and the neighborhood we were in. The Lord was showing me how worthless my self-effort was.

Looking at the small group of people, I thought, "Lord, help me." They started worship, using only a tape player with two singers to lead worship. I said to the Lord, "Give me eyes to see what You are saying here."

At that very moment, I heard the Holy Spirit say, "It can never be about the money or your reputation."

After hearing this, I sat next to Grace and said, "Honey, I am sorry for the way I have viewed this trip." I began to tell her what the Lord was saying to me about faith and motives. She agreed wholeheartedly, and we prayed together in our little metal folding chairs and told God we would not make ministry about the money.

After worship, the pastor introduced me, and the Lord moved mightily in that service through words of knowledge, prophetic words, and salvation. The prophetic word for the city and church was later confirmed to us after I spoke it. At the end of the event, a sweet little old woman walked up to Grace and me and said she had a word to share with us. This woman was their prophet, and she had a heart of gold. We began praying, and she said she had been asked by the pastor to pray for us, and she was so nervous because she thought, "Lord, what can I do?" She said she felt silly even giving the word she had received from the Lord.

I told her, "You have to give it if it's from God, because He knows what's best in relation to what we need."

So she said as she watched us walk into the church, she heard the Lord say, "I want you to tell them I said, 'Thank you.'"

Of course, by this time Grace and I were in tears, because we understood what she was releasing. It wasn't just that the Lord was saying thank you for coming to this small church and giving your all. He was saying something even bigger than that to us that day, and it was, "Thank you for saying yes to My invitation of humility and having the right heart motives."

SEEING THROUGH EYES OF LOVE

God loves it when we are motivated by love rather than economy or a desire to be great for our own name's sake. By His grace, I saw those people at that church with the love of the Holy Spirit, and that became the reason I ministered the way I did. I didn't minister well so I could take up a large offering or be looked at as a powerful man of God. Rather, my heart was motivated by a desire to see the people ministered to and set free. That is love, that is Jesus, and that is the whole point.

PEOPLE EVERYWHERE WANT TO BE KNOWN AND LOVED AS THEY REALLY ARE.

In the years I have spent as a counselor, I have met many people who have different motives for why they do what they do. Some people perform so they will be accepted, hoping acceptance will grow into love. Others don't make any effort at all because of their wounds and self-defeating thoughts. But all the people I have counseled have one thing in common—they all want love and want to be viewed with the eyes of love. No matter what culture we live in, people have basic needs, and one of these basic needs is love. People everywhere want to be known and loved as they really are. All people want to be known, but because of the difficulties of this life, many people become hidden. Some of the most selfish, deceived, and broken people I have met at the very core of who they are just really want to be loved by God and others. This is how God designed us, and it is the key to reaching people's hearts. Only love—His love—is the answer.

To see others with the eyes of love is to ask how Jesus views them. Jesus loves others perfectly and never once fails in anything He sets out to do. The beautiful thing is that through Jesus we can view others exactly as He does. We can see through His lens. Because of Jesus's death and resurrection, our failures and weakness are eclipsed by His perfection, and He has made everything He did available to us so we can spread the kingdom. This means we can see like He sees and be motivated only by love in all we do.

The two most important commandments in the Bible have to do with our ability to see others through Jesus's lens:

> "Teacher, which is the greatest commandment in the law?" Jesus said to him, "'You shall love the Lord your God with all your heart, and with all your soul, and with all your mind.' This is the first and great commandment. And the second is like it: 'You shall love your neighbor as your-self.' On these two commandments hang all the Law and the Prophets."
> —MATTHEW 22:36–40, MEV

Jesus answered the question about which was the great commandment by quoting Deuteronomy 6:5: "You shall love the LORD your God with all your heart." Then He added three new ideas. First, loving God is the first and greatest thing. Second, loving people is like loving God. Third, the purpose of God, as seen in Scripture, hangs on (or originates from) these commandments. The greatest anointing of the Spirit comes from walking in the two great commandments by loving Jesus with all our hearts and loving our neighbors as ourselves. In this way, love becomes our center and the motive for all we do.

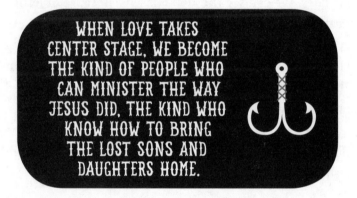

WHEN LOVE TAKES CENTER STAGE, WE BECOME THE KIND OF PEOPLE WHO CAN MINISTER THE WAY JESUS DID, THE KIND WHO KNOW HOW TO BRING THE LOST SONS AND DAUGHTERS HOME.

If we put the second commandment first, our ministry becomes an idol in our hearts. The bottom line is, people who love Jesus will love others much more. It is impossible to love Jesus and not love people more. But when love takes center stage, we become the kind of people who can minister the way Jesus did, the kind who know how to bring the lost sons and daughters home.

Chapter 14

THE WHOLE PACKAGE

T HE GREATEST COMMANDMENT, JESUS SAID, IS this: "You shall love the Lord your God with all your heart, and with all your soul, and with all your mind, and with all your strength" (Mark 12:30, MEV). In this final chapter I want to look more closely at what it means to love God with our hearts, souls, minds, and strength—with the whole package of who we are. Love is the foundation we build our lives on. Who or what we love most determines who we will become and how we will minister to others. Love is how the prodigals find themselves and step into freedom. It's how the children of God demonstrate Father God's heart in a way that compels the lost to come back home. Loving God with all we are will change everything, and it will enable us to truly love ourselves and truly love others.

God created us to love Him in these four distinct spheres of our lives—heart, soul, mind, and strength. God created us to love Him in this way because this is how He loves us. What an incredible truth—God loves us with all His heart, soul, mind, and strength! Of course, love does not automatically develop in these spheres without our involvement. We are responsible to steward its growth.

In chapter 22 of his Gospel, Matthew added another sentence to Jesus's statement that Mark omitted. In verse 38, Jesus said, "This is the first commandment and this is the great commandment" (my paraphrase). It is the first commandment because it is God's first priority. It is the first emphasis of the Holy Spirit in our lives. It is always first on His agenda, the thing He is doing first in the church. Loving God is also the greatest commandment. Our obedience to it has the greatest impact on God's heart. It moves His heart, and it impacts our hearts. And the overflow of loving God deeply impacts the people we love.

Loving God with all we are is also the greatest calling. I have talked to many people who are anxious to discover God's will for their lives. When asked about God's will for their lives, they are mostly focused on what are they supposed to do. But the will of God for our lives—although it certainly does involve doing things—is first about what we are supposed to become, not what we are supposed to do. When I meet someone who says, "I am struggling to find the will of God," I think, "I already know the primary will of God for your life: the first commandment. It is the first priority." People primarily focus on what they are supposed to do, but God does not care about that as much. Who we are supposed to become is more important. Only when we become who we are supposed to become will our deeds have kingdom impact.

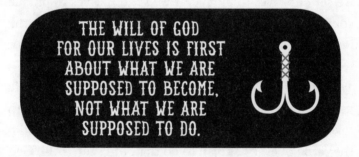

THE WILL OF GOD FOR OUR LIVES IS FIRST ABOUT WHAT WE ARE SUPPOSED TO BECOME, NOT WHAT WE ARE SUPPOSED TO DO.

ALL OUR HEARTS

Let's start by examining how to love God with all our hearts. Simply put, it means loving God in a way that involves and touches our emotions. It is not just a cold, distant, obedient, dutiful servanthood. It is not being involved in a program of ministering to people in a dutiful and responsible way. We are to love God in a way that affects and stirs our emotions. I am not talking about emotionalism. I am not talking about stirring us up, but I am talking about consciously doing what is in the Word of God, which increases our desire for God.

The Bible makes it clear that we have a significant role in determining how our emotions develop over time. Some imagine that whatever happens in their emotions just happens, but we actually have a significant involvement in the development of our emotions and how we feel. It takes a while to change our emotions, but we can change them. Our emotions will follow whatever we set ourselves to pursue. If we set ourselves to pursue something, our emotions will be more attached to it the longer we pursue it. That is just how the human spirit works.

When Jesus said, "Love Me with all your heart," He meant, "Love Me in a way that causes your emotions to take hold of Me and to connect with Me." It is within the reach of every human to do that. In Psalm 91:14, God talks about the person who sets his love on God. If we set our love on Him, our desire for love will increase. We need to make loving Him an object of focus and go after it. Loving God in a general sense is not enough. We need to set our love on Him and say, "Lord, I want my heart and my emotions to be engaged in my pursuit of You."

I am not talking about how we express our emotions in a meeting. I am talking about the way our hearts engage with God. As we change our minds, the Spirit will change our emotions. We have the power to change our minds, and the Spirit will change our emotions according to what we do with our minds. This is how we change our emotions: we set our minds on pursuing God, and our emotions will follow in time.

ALL OUR MINDS

The second sphere of loving God is our minds. We love Him with our minds by filling our minds with thoughts that inspire love for God (instead of thoughts that diminish love for God). Our minds are the doorway to our inner selves. What we do with our minds greatly affects our capacity to love. If we fill our minds with the right things, our capacity to love increases. If we fill our minds with wrong things, our capacity to love diminishes.

Much of our lives actually occurs in our minds. Our minds, which are going twenty-four hours a day, are like a vast universe within. We will be learning and remembering things for billions of years, and we will never exhaust the capacity of our minds, even in the resurrection. In this age many layers exist in the natural mind. And we cannot recall most of what is in that big hard drive called "the human mind." It is a vast universe. It can never be turned off—ever.

The language of the human spirit is images. When someone says, "Pink elephant," we do not think of the concept. We instantly picture a pink elephant. Our minds are internal movie screens that continually show pictures. They are always running and will run forever. They will never stop. When we sleep, we recognize a fraction of 1 percent of the images—we call those dreams. But we are never aware of the vast majority of the images in our minds.

For billions of years, the images can never be shut down, but they can be directed. The images can be changed. We can replace the dark thoughts with new ones, and we can rewrite the movie script that plays on the inside. After all, we are the producer, the main star, and the consumer in that movie script. We produce it, we act in it, and we watch it.

Many believers are very casual about what they do with their minds. Yet the mind is a glorious and powerful reality with vast potential. So many believers fill their minds with entertainment and waste their time daydreaming about vanity. This is disheartening, because they have the Holy Spirit and a Bible and the kingdom of God. The Lord is saying, "Love Me with your mind. Do not fill your mind with so much entertainment, and do not be so absorbed in daydreaming about vanity. Take hold of the reins of your mind. Read the Word of God. Love Me with your mind."

ALL OUR STRENGTH

Third, we love God with all our strength. This includes both our natural strength and our natural resources—our money, our time, our physical energy, and our words. We express love for God by the way we choose to invest our resources. When we give God our strength, or our resources, we express our love for God in a way that is meaningful to Him. When we pour out our strength for Him, God takes it personally. He takes it as an act of love, because it is costly for us to give our resources to Him. It costs us something. We lose something in the natural when we give our resources to Him. Of course, He always returns them. He multiplies them and returns them, but for that moment we actually lose them. We do this because we love Him, and He takes it personally. He smiles and He says, "I like that."

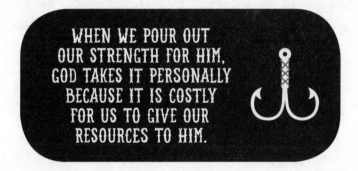

WHEN WE POUR OUT OUR STRENGTH FOR HIM, GOD TAKES IT PERSONALLY BECAUSE IT IS COSTLY FOR US TO GIVE OUR RESOURCES TO HIM.

Hebrews 6:10 says God will not forget the love we show toward Him when we do things for other people. When we pour out our strength for others, we are actually showing love to Him, and He sees it that way. Normally, people use their resources to increase their own personal comfort and honor. All of us use our time, money, and words to obtain more honor and possessions.

There is nothing wrong with that. We are supposed to do this, but we are not supposed to use *all* our strengths that way. Part of our strength we are to give away. We are to sow it as an act of love for God. When we give it away, choosing to actually lose it temporarily because of our love for Him, He receives it as a statement of love.

Every time we invest our strength into our relationship with Him or into His purposes, He sees it. When we sow our time, money, or physical energy, we are sowing it into God's bank, so to speak. God takes careful record of it. He values it, and then He returns it to us, but multiplied. When we give Him our time, we are giving Him some of our effectiveness and productivity. And we are giving Him a chance to increase our influence.

This reality is fleshed out in the principle of the fasted lifestyle, which is found in 2 Corinthians 12:9:

> But he said to me, "My grace is sufficient for you, for my power is made perfect in weakness." Therefore I will boast all the more gladly of my weaknesses, so that the power of Christ may rest upon me.

Paul was suffering persecution, and he was pained over it. People were slandering him and telling lies about him. They were undermining his ministry and hindering his income. He was even beaten with whips and imprisoned. Every time he turned around, something was coming against him. Then the Lord appeared to him and said, "Paul, let Me explain something to you. My grace is sufficient for you, because My strength will be perfected in you as you continue in weakness."

Here, the Lord was not talking about moral weakness but about voluntarily embracing weakness in the choices Paul was making. It meant that if Paul walked into a specific city and preached, he would get beaten up. He knew it. But he walked in and preached anyway, and he didn't fight back when they beat him. In other words, he willingly embraced weakness in terms of his productivity and strength. He embraced the fasted lifestyle to allow Christ's strength to shine through him. We fast our strength in five main ways, as taught by Jesus in the Sermon on the Mount—by serving, by giving money, by praying (because that is an investment of time), by blessing our adversaries (speaking words of blessing instead of words to put our adversaries in their place), and by fasting food.

When we give a couple hours of our time in prayer—time is productivity—sitting in a room and telling God what He tells us to tell Him, that is pouring out our strength to Him. We are giving strength away in the form of our time and productivity. Likewise, when we give our money, we are giving our strength and our ability to influence. We actually really lose it. When we give one hundred dollars, that one hundred dollars really leaves the bank account. And when we love the Lord like this, it is as if the Lord says back to us, "In My accounting system, I will return the financial strength you have lost. I will return what you have lost in productivity by giving

Me your time. I will return everything back to you in My timing."

WHEN WE GIVE OUR TIME IN PRAYER, WE ARE POURING OUT OUR STRENGTH TO HIM.

Fasting food is not really about hunger. It is mostly about physical weakness. We are hungry for a day or two when we fast, but then the compelling hunger lifts. The far bigger problem with fasting is that we are emotionally, mentally, and physically wobbly. Fasting is about physical weakness, because when we do it, we do not have the same ability or clarity of mind. Our emotions get wobbly, our minds get wobbly, and our bodies get wobbly. We really give our strength to the Lord when we do that. Serving people is also a form of fasting. When we serve people, we really lose time and energy. We could use that same time and energy to enrich our own lives, but instead we give our time and energy to God, and we will never get back—except that God returns it in His own way later.

He receives the gift of our strength as love and says to us, "I take it very personally that you have invested yourself in this way." This is what it means to love God with our strength. When we pour out what God has already put inside us, God releases His strength— His grace. When He refers to grace in 2 Corinthians

12:9—"My grace is sufficient for you"—the word *grace* means "God's enabling power."[1] We talked about the other facet of grace earlier in this book, the mercy of God or His unmerited favor. This mercy is a subunit of grace, but the bigger picture of grace is God's empowerment in our lives. The Lord was saying, in effect, "My enabling of you is sufficient. If you will lean on Me, you will experience greater empowerment. You will see an increase called perfected strength."

All Our Souls

Fourth, we are called to love God with all our souls. Our ability to love God with our souls is directly connected to how we derive our identity. This is because our identity is determined by how we define success and value, by how we see ourselves. The most natural way we define success is by our accomplishments. We find our feeling of success in the approval of others. But the Lord wants us to find our identity and our definition of success in our relationship with Him instead of in our accomplishments or our relationships with other people. This is what it means to love Him with our souls. We naturally and automatically find our identity in what we accomplish and who recognizes us, but God is inviting us on a journey of radically shifting the way we define success and therefore the way we derive our identity. He wants us to see and evaluate ourselves through His lens alone.

> THE LORD WANTS US TO
> FIND OUR IDENTITY AND
> OUR DEFINITION OF SUCCESS
> IN OUR RELATIONSHIP
> WITH HIM INSTEAD OF IN
> OUR ACCOMPLISHMENTS
> OR OUR RELATIONSHIPS
> WITH OTHER PEOPLE.

This is Christianity 101, a foundation of our faith we must constantly be reminded of. God's love for us is what determines our personal worth. We are worth so much simply because God chose us and He loves us. When we truly believe this and respond to His love and love Him back, we are loving Him with our souls. That is not a small thing; it is not an automatic thing. Of the seven billion people on the earth, only about two billion, according to the statistics, profess Christianity.[2] That leaves about four billion people who do not know God. That means we are in the significant minority, not only in this time period but in all of history. We are part of the minority to whom God said, "I love you," and by the grace of God, we said, "I will take it, and I will return it. I will love You too." That is what makes our lives successful in the most profound sense.

We need to be anchored in the truth that our success and worth are based on His love for us and our love for Him. They are *not* based on our accomplishments, recognition, possessions, and relationships. That is how people seek after identity in the natural, but it is a really broken system. Because of our natural mind-sets and the darkness of our minds apart from Christ, almost everyone's first response—unless they unlearn it—is to feel rejected and neglected by people. The whole human race feels this way. If we get our identity from being recognized by people, our default will be to feel rejected and neglected and become emotionally damaged in the process. Then our accomplishments will seem so small and so unnoticed that we will not like them.

Most people look at their accomplishments and despise them because they seem so insignificant. They are in a crisis of identity, and it creates a storm of emotional traffic on the inside, a constant preoccupation with trying to find some way of feeling valuable.

Some time ago I learned to start declaring God's approval of me when I came under pressure. When pressure hits, it makes us ask big questions. Pressure tends to make us philosophical, and we start asking, "Why am I even doing this?" When I found myself asking this question, I would tell myself, "The Genesis 1 God, the only one who has Genesis 1 on His résumé, likes me— the Genesis 1 God. Wow!" And I would start to feel like I had it made.

But the Lord stopped me and said, "That is not it. It is not enough that I *like* you. I want you to respond and to love Me. If I love you, and you love Me, you are already successful."

Going through the philosophical questions, I could feel the pressure, and the only way I could land with comfort was by saying, "I am loved by God, and I am a lover of God. Therefore, I am already successful. I made it! Everything else is icing on the cake. I have already made it!" Then I would be happy. When we feel successful, everything else—the relationships, the money, the difficulties, the problems, and the resistance—comes into perspective.

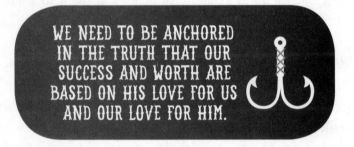

WE NEED TO BE ANCHORED IN THE TRUTH THAT OUR SUCCESS AND WORTH ARE BASED ON HIS LOVE FOR US AND OUR LOVE FOR HIM.

Having the correct perspective on our lives is also the key to avoiding burnout, because burnout does not come from hard work but from working with a wrong spirit. We will not get burned out because we work long hours. We will get burned out because we are working long hours with a wrong spirit—working to become successful at the heart level. When we work in order to become successful, the work will burn us out. If we work because we already are successful, the work will actually strengthen our spirits. If we work from success, we get renewed, but if we work to become successful, we get burned out. I can spend long hours engaged in ministry, and I can be involved in difficult problems in people's lives, if in my core I already know I am successful. But if I am doing the work so I can prove I should be in ministry, that work will burn me out, and I will become disillusioned.

The Lord wants us to shift the way we get our identity. This is how we love God with our souls, to get our identity from our relationship with Him and not from what we produce with our hands or who recognizes us. It is a journey to make that identity shift. It is not a one-day decision. We make the decision one day, and then we go on a journey to stick with it.

I have been on that journey for years, and sometimes I lose my way and become philosophical. The only way I get my comfort is by saying, "I am loved by God, and I am a lover of God; therefore, I am successful. My problem is not that big because my spirit is happy now." When we have a right identity, it removes so much of the emotional traffic. We can love God far better with a clear spirit. I believe this is what Jesus meant when He told us to love Him with all our souls.

Looking back over my life, I am amazed at how much God has allowed me to see and how He has inspired me and healed me of old graves and cradles. By *old graves* I mean the parts of my past that I hadn't truly released myself from, and by *cradles* I mean the immaturity the Lord is working to full maturity. We all are on this journey to giving and receiving love, to becoming dispensers of the kingdom who will partner with our Father in bringing the lost sons and daughters back home. We should never forget where we have come from—that we are simply filthy fishermen saved and redeemed by a loving Father. And with that in view, we should fix our eyes on our destiny in Christ Jesus—to love God with our whole selves and to live out that love in all we do. What a hurricane of love; what an offensive grace; what an implausible restoration. It is our glorious privilege.

SWEET VICTORY

O N December 22, 2008, I married the girl of my dreams—literally. In sixth grade I dreamt of her, this beautiful Asian girl with long, jet-black hair. Her name is Grace, and she is the personification of grace in my life. We had a whirlwind romance and were married less than a year after our first date.

When I was in my pigpen, I never believed I would have a beautiful, sweet wife who would love me and be faithful to me. Honestly I thought I would die in my pigpen. But God had other plans; His grace stepped in. He broke into my pigpen and pulled me out.

My wedding day felt bittersweet, as I stood at the altar in front of our closest friends and family. Here was Grace, a beautiful woman who had saved herself for me. She was so worthy of my purity! My heart grieved that I had not listened to all those "purity promise" messages! I cried, seeing the Lord's goodness stand before me. And then He reminded me that I too was a gift to Grace.

Today I have a beautiful wife; the most beautiful daughter on the planet, Gemma; a home; and an RV that was given to our family as a mode of ministry transportation. When I was a prodigal, I never imagined I could have any of these things. And every day I look at my daughter as a reminder of where I came from.

My life is proof that God can do the miraculous and impossible. When all hope seemed lost for my parents and me, God stepped in. And now I'm living my God-given destiny, which was spoken over me and knit into me while I was still in my mother's womb. It's the very destiny the enemy tried so hard to destroy.

If you are a prodigal, it's not too late for you to turn around. Nothing the world can offer you will come even remotely close to the destiny God has for you. Let Him redeem and restore you in the way that only He can. Quit trying to wrestle your own way out of quicksand, and let Him be God. Let your Savior save you.

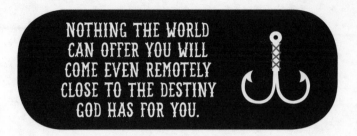

NOTHING THE WORLD CAN OFFER YOU WILL COME EVEN REMOTELY CLOSE TO THE DESTINY GOD HAS FOR YOU.

If you are struggling with a prodigal, don't give up. Resolve in your heart that you will not give up until there is no breath left—either in you or in your prodigal. Get tenacious with your prayers, and place a demand on the promises God has made you! Keep loving bravely, but don't forget that your job is to pray and God's job is to bring change. It's a marathon, so pace yourself with much patience.

NOTES

CHAPTER 2
BITTERSWEET DESTINY

1.   Greek Dictionary (Lexicon-Concordance) G1650, *elegchos*, and G1651, *elegchō*, Lexicon-Concordance Online Bible, accessed November 5, 2015, http://lexiconcordance .com/greek/165.html.

CHAPTER 3
FOREFATHERS OF FAILURE

1.   As quoted in John Stott, *Basic Christian Leadership: Biblical Models of Church, Gospel and Ministry* (Chicago, IL: InterVarsity Press, 2002), 47.

2.   Hebrew Dictionary (Lexicon-Concordance) H7343, *Rachab*, Lexicon-Concordance Online Bible, accessed November 5, 2015, http://lexiconcordance.com/hebrew/7343 .html.

CHAPTER 4
FILTHY FISHERMEN

1.   I have read in various sources that this is common Hebrew custom when choosing a new rabbi to be trained.

2.   Blue Letter Bible G2480, *ischyō*, accessed November 11, 2015, http://www.blueletterbible.org/lang/Lexicon/Lexicon .cfm?strongs=G2480&t=KJV.

3. Greek Dictionary (Lexicon-Concordance) G2560, kakōs, Lexicon-Concordance Online Bible, accessed November 5, 2015, http://lexiconcordance.com/greek/2560.html. The idea is that if you have grief in this regard, you're either causing it for others or you're receiving it.

CHAPTER 6
OFFENSIVE GRACE

1. Charles Spurgeon, "God's Goodness Leading to Repentance" (sermon, Metropolitan Tabernacle, London, England, November 18, 1877), accessed November 11, 2015, http://www.spurgeongems.org/vols49-51/chs2857.pdf.

2. Greek Dictionary (Lexicon-Concordance) G3811, *paideuo*, Lexicon-Concordance Online Bible, November 5, 2015, http://lexiconcordance.com/greek/3811.html.

CHAPTER 7
PRAY FOR DAYLIGHT

1. As quoted in Greg Laurie, *New Believer's Guide to Prayer* (Wheaton, IL: Tyndale, 2003).

2. Bob Sorge, *Secrets of the Secret Place* (Grandview, MO: Oasis House, 2001), 49.

3. Ibid.

CHAPTER 8
HURRICANE LOVE

1. The names and certain identifying details of the people referenced in this chapter have been changed to protect the privacy of the individuals and their families.

CHAPTER 9
IMPLAUSIBLE RESTORATION

1. Dictionary.com, s.v. "restoration," *Dictionary.com Unabridged*, Random House, Inc., accessed September 14, 2015, http://dictionary.reference.com/browse/restoration.

2. Thesaurus.com, s.v. "restoration," *Roget's 21st Century Thesaurus, Third Edition* (Princeton, NJ: Philip Lief Group, 2009), accessed September 14, 2015, http://www.thesaurus.com/browse/restoration.

CHAPTER 11
THE MASTERPIECE

1. Bob Sorge, *Power of the Blood* (Grandview, MO: Oasis House, 2008), 11.

2. If we become like Christ as we behold Him, then we can also become like the negative things we worship. To worship means to give our attention and hearts to something.

CHAPTER 14
THE WHOLE PACKAGE

1. Harold W. Hoehner, *Ephesians: An Exegetical Commentary* (Grand Rapids, MI: Baker Academic, 2002), 450.

2. "Christians," Pew-Templeton Global Religious Futures Project, accessed November 5, 2015, http://www.globalreligiousfutures.org/religions/christians.

ABOUT LUKE HOLTER

Luke Holter is the founder and senior director of Prophetic Sheep Ministries and The Samuel Institute, which aims to establish a healthy prophetic culture in the church by raising up prophets and prophetic voices through education, relationship, and accountability. Luke is an in-demand speaker and the award-winning author of *A Beautiful Kind of Broken*. As a prophetic messenger, he travels extensively for conferences, international missions, and leadership training. He and his wife, Grace, partner and serve with a growing number of churches and ministries, often crossing denominational lines, to manifest the love of God in the church locally and abroad.

CONNECT WITH US!

CHARISMA HOUSE

(Spiritual Growth)

f Facebook.com/CharismaHouse

y @CharismaHouse

◉ Instagram.com/CharismaHouseBooks

SILOAM

(Health)

ⓟ Pinterest.com/CharismaHouse

REALMS

(Fiction)

f Facebook.com/RealmsFiction